This book belongs to

Fred Dibnah

Fred Dibnah
The Early Days

It seems almost incredible that 30 years have passed since we first saw Fred Dibnah on our television screens. This unlikely celebrity captivated us with his amazing feats of bravery as he swung on a rope 200ft long whilst inspecting a factory chimney, or ran for his life as he demolished a chimney, with hundreds of ton of bricks tumbling down around him.

Always cheery, you couldn't help but be drawn into Fred's life, as each week millions of eager television viewers awaited the next documentary to be shown on BBC 2.

Without doubt, Fred Dibnah was a one off. From an early age he had dreams of being a steeplejack, something that he accomplished without any formal training. He didn't learn his trade by working with other steeplejacks, he taught himself by trial and error and became one of the best.

It is not surprising that television came looking for Fred. His manner, his job and his hobby made him an interesting subject.

This beautifully presented bookazine covers the period when Fred was at his pinnacle. A period where fame had not affected him. He knew he was famous, but he thought the television people would come and go, and that he would be remembered as a steeplejack. A good one at that.

'Fred Dibnah The Early Days' is totally written by Fred in his own words, and tells his life story up to when the television cameras came and made their first documentary three decades ago.

Compiled using rare, original photographs and documents, we present you with a true and accurate look in to the lives of one of Britain's greatest heroes.

Compiled and researched by Paul Donoghue
Art Editor: Rob Callaghan
All photographs and documents are taken from The Paul Donoghue Heritage collection.
Design/Illustrations: Trevor Hamlett, Brian Smith
Reformatting of the original Fred Dibnah Steeplejack book by kind permission of Peter Nicholson.
Website: www.freddibnah.tv

Digital Production Manager: Nicky Baker

Management
Bookazine Manager: Dharmesh Mistry
Production Director: Robin Ryan
Managing Director of Advertising: Julian Lloyd-Evans
Newstrade Director: Martin Belson
Chief Operating Officer: Brett Reynolds
Group Finance Director: Ian Leggett
Chief Executive: James Tye
Chairman: Felix Dennis

Magbook
The "Magbook" brand is a trademark of Dennis Publishing Ltd. 30 Cleveland St, London W1T 4JD. Company registered in England. All material © Paul Donoghue & Dennis Publishing Ltd, licensed by Felden 2009, and may not be reproduced in whole or part without the consent of the publishers.
Fred Dibnah The Early Days, ISBN 978-1-907232-00-8

Licensing
To license this product, please contact Winnie Liesenfeld on +44 (0) 20 7907 6134 or email winnie_liesenfeld@dennis.co.uk

Liability
While every care was taken during the production of this Magbook, the publishers cannot be held responsible for the accuracy of the information or any consequence arising from it. Dennis Publishing takes no responsibility for the companies advertising in this Magbook.

The paper used within this Magbook is produced from sustainable fibre, manufactured by mills with a valid chain of custody. Printed at Polestar

MAG**BOOK**

Dr Frederick Dibnah MBE 1938 - 2004

"eight gives you a wonderful
ing of grandeur. You're the
king of the castle up here."

"I realise that steam engines aren't everyone's cup of tea. But they're what made England great."

Steam through the unique
beauty of Brontë Country

Every weekend and daily
throughout the summer

Special Events run
throughout the year including
Steam Galas, Vintage Trains, Dining Trains,
Cream Teas, Diesel Weekend, Beer & Music Festival,
Santa Steam Specials and Mince Pie Specials

David R Carr

WORTH VALLEY .... one of Britain's Ten Best Train Trips (The Sunday Times)

THE KEIGHLEY & WORTH VALLEY RAILWAY PRESERVATION SOCIETY

The Railway Station, Haworth, Keighley, West Yorkshire BD22 8NJ
Telephone 01535 645214   www.kwvr.co.uk
Keep up to date with the KWVR 24hr Info 01535 647777

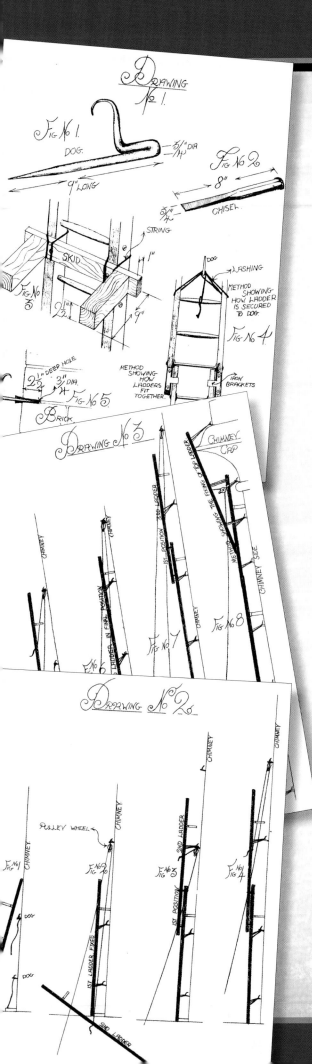

Contents

Foreword
By Paul Donoghue

When you look back and analyse the life of this country's most famous steeplejack and steam man, you would be amazed at just how much Frederick Dibnah M.B.E. managed to achieve in his 66 years of life.

If the reader has the time to study Fred Dibnah and can arm themselves with some of the mountains of information that is available via the internet, films, newspaper archives or books, they could have a fantastic time following in the footsteps of the great man.

Fred certainly left his mark, and there are many examples of his work that we can still see today. It's also true to say that Fred singlehandedly rid the Lancashire landscape of some of its most spectacular landmarks.

Illustration of Fred preparing a weathervane for the top of a church spire.

Fred enjoying a pint of beer during an extended lunch break...

I recently spent some time with former boiler maker, turned historian and author Alan McEwen. We were both lucky enough to have been present at Fred Dibnah's demolition of the chimney at the former Monton Mill at Eccles, Manchester on Sunday 4th August 1991. I was there to film the day's proceedings, and Alan (at Fred's request) had come along to capture the demolition with his stills cameras. Neither I nor Alan was introduced on the day, but fascinatingly we could both have gone on Mastermind and got top marks if our specialist subject happened to be the Monton Mill Chimney Drop. Anyway, I've started so I'll finish. When Alan and I returned to the site at Eccles, engaged in some filming work and interviews, the whole place had changed beyond our recognition. What was (in 1991) an industrial and demolition site had evolved into a housing estate with an array of flats, apartments and houses all with well-kept gardens.

We could both have gone on Mastermind and got top marks if our specialist subject had been the Monton Mill Chimney Drop.

Fred Dibnah
The Early Days

At some stage, Alan and I decided that we would attempt to locate the exact position of where the chimney had stood all those years ago. Easy, you might think. Wrong. It took us almost two hours of pacing up and down the streets using photographs and our memory before we eventually agreed that we found the spot. So if you have some spare time and want to locate exactly where the Monton Chimney stood, I will make it easy for you. It's car park plot E7, outside Waterfront House on Monton Mill Gardens. Or if you have GPS, it's latitude 53°29'24.20"N longitude 2°21'32.08"W.

Fred Dibnah left behind many other things we can look at: chimney stacks, weathervanes, steam engines, his yard, and his meticulous restoration projects. Then there are his books, DVDs and his unmissable BBC series that spanned almost three decades. Fred has also been honoured by the people of his hometown, Bolton, where a huge bronze statue of him holding a lightning conductor stands proudly in the town centre. For those who want to pay personal respects, you can visit his final resting place at the much visited grave in Tongue cemetery, only 500 yards from the rear of his house on Radcliffe Road.

Fred Dibnah was one of the wittiest people I have ever met. I have seen Ken Dodd, Bob Monkhouse, Charlie Williams and the like, and Fred was certainly in this class had he chosen to be a performer. His delivery of a punch line was second to none. Listening to one of his tales or stories would have you and any audience in stitches and fits of laughter. His stage shows completely sold out across the country, and the irony of it all was that Fred was simply telling stories about his life as a steeplejack – there were no jokes! You can experience this yourself by listening to his favourite stories on the cover CD of this publication.

Fred with mug in hand and a cheery smile.
He liked coffee and never drank tea.

Alan McEwen on the search for the Monton Chimney site.

A collection of family photographs from one of Fred's private albums.

One of my funniest recollections is when I was interviewing Fred and asked him how far back the method of propping up chimneys with wood and then setting them alight went. Scratching his chin, Fred went into great detail of how it was first introduced during the battle of Jericho in 9000BC and that Joshua ordered his men to tunnel under the Jordan River and start removing the stone foundations of the great city walls and prop the gaps with timber and chocks. Fred continued with a wry smile, I'm not sure where they got all the wood from with all the deserts in the area, but when they eventually lit the fire, as history has proved, the walls came tumbling down.

I had to endure other wind-ups like the steeplejack who was struck by lightning, lost his leg, but was back at work on Bolton's biggest chimney stack within six months with a tin leg. Not to mention the gripping story of the day Fred nearly died when he fell in a puddle that turned out to be a 5ft deep flue full of water as the chimney was just about to topple. "How did you get out Fred?" I asked. "I don't know lad, but it must have been an incredible fart to get me out of there. It were nearly half a day out with the undertaker, I can tell you that for sure," he replied.

When I was with Fred Dibnah, I always felt that he knew that he wasn't going to live to an incredible age. In a dark way he would hint that he felt that he wasn't going to be here long, that the clock of life would beat him. "I've got so much to do and I'm running out of time," he would say. "Chimney stacks are made to cause pollution, and I have sucked in more smoke, soot and ash in a day than some people breathe in a whole lifetime, so something will have to give – I am sure of that." It is perhaps for this reason that Fred Dibnah (in his own mind) felt he had to leave his mark. I am sure that deep down he knew he was someone special and that he would eventually be immortalised. In particular, I remember Fred giving a press interview after the Farnworth chimney drop (18th October 1991). The reporter asked Fred how he would like to be remembered, and Fred replied "As Fred Dibnah Steeplejack from Bolton." We all know that Fred Dibnah was much more than that.

Following the huge success of Fred Dibnah's first BBC documentary, the public wanted to know more about

Fred Dibnah on the footplate of his beloved steam roller, up to his cap in oil and grease.

the flat-cap wearing, steam-roller driving, chimney demolisher and daredevil from Bolton.

It was at this time that Fred was approached to put pen to paper and write his life story. During the negotiations to write his first book, Fred insisted that he wanted the book to be written completely in his own words, style and dialect. Fred also told the authors that they had to make sure that the book (when in print) was just as he had written it, and that he wanted the reader to feel like he had written them a personal letter.

When completed, the book was given the same title as Fred's first television documentary, 'Fred Dibnah Steeplejack'. Unsurprisingly, the book became an instant success with the buying public and within weeks 'Fred Dibnah Steeplejack' was a best seller.

Three decades after its first release, 'Fred Dibnah Steeplejack' has become a rare and collectable item. Copies of the book signed by Fred regularly sell for £100 or more.

Fred always told me that his early books were his favourites. So with the use of my original document and photograph archive I give you an up-to-date edition of Fred's best-selling literary masterpiece.

Chimney stacks are made to cause pollution, and I have sucked in more smoke, soot and ash in a day than some people breathe in a whole lifetime

Chapter one
The Early years

When I was a little lad, I went to school like all little lads do. In those days the main road from Bolton to Manchester was made of blue cobbled stones and had two tram tracks down middle. I never liked going to school so me mother used to shove me on a tram, which then went rattling along the road. For the next mile and a half there were five chimney stacks to be counted and where I got off stood a great mass of them belching black smoke.

Every so often, ladders painted bright red with men going up and down them appeared on the chimneys. When you are seven years old, a man at the top of a 200ft high stack looks like someone from outer space. Those fellows really fascinated me, though the only two facts I knew about them were that they had red ladders and wore flat caps. Then one morning after prayers, our headmaster announced he had a special treat for us kids. We were going to watch one of them great chimneys fall.

In strict single file we were marched to a field at the back of the school and told to sit perfectly still. I remember we sat all morning, full of tension, waiting for that chimney to topple. It were still standing when we went home for midday dinner. On our return to school, the stack lay on the ground and we had missed everything...

"I never saw it come down,"
I told my parents. "I never did."

The earliest known photograph of Fred Dibnah, aged 5 months.

An early example of a chimney felling. Similar to the one that Fred Dibnah and the rest of his class mates missed.

My school days rolled on and I kept seeing more red ladders appearing on the chimneys around me. I never knew who owned them until years later. By then, me father had an allotment beside a greyhound track on a site which had once been occupied by an old colliery. The old colliery chimney was still standing and the chap who owned the site (which also had dog kennels and a cafe) decided it were time to get rid of the stack.

He engaged the services of some sort of mountain men from a place called Bacup near Todmorden. These characters arrived with ladders that had once been red but were now very wishy-washy. The men began by knocking off the top of the chimney. After that they chopped a big hole in the bottom and put in blocks of wood. I did not know what was going on, though that were no matter. You see I had a ringside seat being allowed in the allotment with me father.

It were a right gloomy Sunday during winter and when the mountain men lit their fire under chimney the flames danced in the dark. The site owner also put on all the lights round his greyhound tracks which made us very excited. Then things began to go wrong. This was because not many chimneys were knocked down in those days and no-one really knew what they were doing. The chimney came down sure enough, but it did not go right. I vividly recall the stack cutting the dog kennels in half and chopping a corner off the cafe. In addition, it ripped down every power cable and all the lights went out. There were utter panic.

A mill chimney being repaired. As a schoolboy Fred Dibnah admired the work of the steeplejacks in flat caps...

School boy Fred in his uniform.

My next craze was to get a bike because everyone else seemed to have one. Even though me father slaved in a bleach factory and me mother at the gas works, we never had any real money. Therefore a bike was something to be made by visiting refuge tips. If you were lucky there would be a frame here and a couple of wheels somewhere else. After that came a pair of handlebars and you did not worry too much about brakes in them days.

The point was my bike enabled me to get about a bit, searching for more things. By a fantastic stroke of luck I found an old pair of binoculars. I would then travel to, and climb on top of the Earl of Bradford's slag heap. From there, on clear summer nights I could survey the edges of Bolton and especially all them chimney stacks. It had to be summer, for in winter you could not see for the heavy smoke.

It were a right gloomy Sunday during winter when the mountain men lit their fire under chimney.

Bright eyed and smartly dressed, Brylcreem on his hair, and wearing a tie and blazer. One of Fred Dibnah's official school photographs.

One clear summer night I spotted some strange black lines across the top of a chimney. They belonged to somebody's staging and next night I cycled right across town to have a closer look at what were going on. As I got near I saw red ladders with the name 'John Faulkner, Manchester' on their sides. Well you know how some fellows follow pop groups or football teams. From that evening my hero was John Faulkner.

I started to follow John Faulkner and his men who climbed chimneys around Bolton and Manchester. To my mind they did things right compared to others. Their staging when it appeared on top of a stack was square, symmetrical and solid looking with ropes coiled up all nice and neat. The others had crooked and funny looking staging with bits of rope blowing in the wind.

This were when I was still at school though not doing very well. I was no good at reading and writing so they put the likes of me in the art group. There we painted vases of flowers and bowls of apples. Also, when our teacher felt like it we would go for walks with our drawing books. Of course, you could not go anywhere without seeing chimneys. Not only did I draw all the chimneys but I put in red ladders and staging.

"What have you put those in for?" my teacher would ask. I answered, "It were in my mind."

My school holidays were spent chimney watching. I always had to go home around about midday and take me father's dinner to the bleach works. He worked in an unbelievable place. Every corner you turned there were a steam engine throbbing away and driving some piece of shafting. They had big steam engines for the main heavy bits and little ones stuck in different places. More steam came out of the roof than went through the pipes and every evening there were adverts in the local paper for boiler stokers.

Me father worked at a contraption called a beetling machine, which were a creation of the devil. If you study a piece of cloth just after weaving, it is full of protruding fibres that have to be flattened. The modern method is

Frank and Betsy Dibnah enjoying some time away. Fred always believed that his parents suffered a life of toil, with his father and mother working in the bleach works and later his mother working in the gas works as a charlady.

to run the cloth through steam-heated rollers, but in them days beetling machines were the norm. They were monstrous, with cast iron frames and rollers, beech beams and oak noggins.

Well you know how some fellows follow pop groups or football teams. From that evening my hero was John Faulkner, Steeplejack.

Also, there were no safety guards round anything. As the big cast iron rollers with all the oak noggins turned, the cloth was dragged through the machine. Apart from the dirt flying about, the noise was terrible and you could not hear yourself speak. No-one can describe what it sounded like, though some literary character called it 'Dante's Inferno'.

I was sent to some funeral parlour where the undertaker looked like a corpse himself.

To think that me father spent 40 uncomplaining years working one of those creations. Below the floor where he worked there were a river alive with rats. They raced about below him and would climb boldly up to have a go at his dinner when I arrived with it. Two big chimneys above the bleach works belched out black smoke day and night. Nowt was ever done about anything as the mill owners were also big on the town council.

When me dad realised I had this strange interest in steeplejacking, he told me the following tale. "During war," he said, "some jacks came to repair tops of chimneys. Well they got up all right and fixed their staging. However, the chimneys were kept working and hot due to the war effort. There must have been thousands of tons of coal burnt below them." "Couldn't have been comfortable up top," I said. "It were not," me father agreed. "One lot of staging went on fire and was all glowing like a beacon in the blackout. Everyone were powerless to do anything about it until the flames fizzled out." "Fantastic!" I said.

But there were no vacancies for would-be steeplejacks or chimney sweeps when I went to the Youth Employment Bureau, as it was called in those days. The chap behind the counter said, "Well now, we have one very good job available. Undertaking." Sometimes I wish I had taken that up because, whatever else happens, undertakers are never out of business.

Anyway, I was sent to some funeral parlour where the undertaker looked like a corpse himself. With a funny sort of smile he opened a door and beckoned me into a room filled with trestles and coffins.

While looking around I thought 'This isn't for me.' So I acted real dumb and was sent back to the Youth Employment Bureau. "Well now," said the chap behind the counter, "we have another good opportunity available as a jobbing joiner. Trouble is, six other lads are after it and they're already walking there." "I have me bike," I said like Norman Tebbit. The joiner gaffer was called Mr. Rawlinson, who later let me call him Bill – God rest his soul. He was a nice man and by way of a test asked me if I knew what a Tenon saw was. I told him me grandfather had left me one of them which went down well.

Well now, said the chap behind the counter, we have another good opportunity available as a jobbing joiner.

A time when the wheels of industry were turning and England was the workshop to the world.

The long and the short of it was I got the job, and for that first four years everything were marvellous. One day, Mr. Rawlinson asked me if I had ever done any pointing. We had just put a window frame in but as for working with mortar he hadn't got a clue.

So after doing the window, I had to point a whole garden wall, which took me about a fortnight. The old woman at whose house I worked was so impressed she asked if I could do the same to her gable ends. They were three stories high and I did not have anything like the tackle needed to get up there. Mr. Rawlinson took me to one side like I was his friend. "I don't want to turn down work," he said. "Can you do it?" "It's elementary steeplejacking," I assured him, "and I've studied all them techniques."

How I managed it with his short ladders and bits of board lashed together I shall never know. I did however, and Mr. Rawlinson realised it were like another extension to his joinery business. He now went in for what he called 'Property Repairing', with me pointing one gable end after another. Yet, as I said, he were a good man and like most others in those days did not have much money. What he did have was an old Worsley Hornet car with a leather body and what they called a sunshine roof. That meant the rain came straight through. Eventually Mr. Rawlinson filled it full of wood shavings from his planing machine, put a sheet of felt over the top and tarred the whole lot. That were high technology for them days.

He also had a trailer with Austin artillery wheels from the 1920s. Mr. Rawlinson never once painted them and the rust had been rampant for years. Although each wheel were made of two metal plates welded together, you could see daylight through both of them. I sort of accepted anything then. There was not even a toilet at his works – you had to pee in a corner of the yard. How we worked was I loaded up the trailer then he drove me to the job. Afterwards, Mr. Rawlinson went elsewhere and I had to find my own way back to the yard.

That was where he made his mistake as far as I were concerned. While working at joinery, I would be studying the nearest chimney, particularly if it had red ladders on it. I still hankered after being a steeplejack in a flat cap, going up and down them red ladders.

But I were employed by Mr. Rawlinson and I worried about his trailer. He did overload it. Sometimes he filled that trailer with six cubic yards of solid wood, all wet through as well.

There was not even a toilet at his works—you had to pee in a corner of the yard.

NATIONAL JOINT COUNCIL FOR THE BUILDING INDUSTRY

DEED OF APPRENTICESHIP.

FORM No. 1

This Deed of Apprenticeship made the 4th day of October 1954 BETWEEN --- William Rawlinson --------

of Bk. Boston Street, Halliwell, Bolton in the County of Lancaster (hereinafter called "the Master") of the first part

-------- Frank Dibnah ----------

of 8 Alfred Street, Bolton aforesaid

------------ (hereinafter called "the Guardian") of the second part

-------- Frederick Dibnah ----------

of 8 Alfred Street, Bolton aforesaid

------------ (hereinafter called "the Apprentice") of the third part

and -------- Arthur Wallwork Talbot --------

of "High-Close", Chorley New Road, Heaton, Bolton aforesaid (hereinafter called "the Representative") of the fourth part.

WHEREAS

(1) The Representative has been selected by the Local Joint Apprenticeship Committee for the Bolton and Farnworth Area of the North Western Region constituted by the National Joint Council for the Building Industry, to be a party to this Deed in accordance with their Scheme of Apprenticeship dated the first day of November, 1945, and

(2) The Apprentice has attained the age of 16 years and is employed on probation by the Master with a view to becoming an apprentice in the Building Industry, and

(3) The Master and the Representative are satisfied that the Apprentice is a suitable person to be taught and instructed as an apprentice in the craft of a Joiner, and

(4) The Guardian and the Representative have enquired into the nature of the business conducted by the Master and desire that the Apprentice should learn the craft of a Joiner in the service of the Master.

NOW THIS DEED WITNESSETH as follows:—

1. The Apprentice of his own free will and with the consent of the Guardian hereby binds himself as Apprentice in the craft of a Joiner and the

Strike out if the Master is not a Limited Company.
IN WITNESS whereof the Common Seal of the party of the first part has hereunto been affixed and the parties of the second third and fourth parts have hereunto set their hands and seals the day and year first above written.

Strike out if the Master is a Limited Company.
IN WITNESS whereof the parties hereto have hereunto set their hands and seals the day and year first above written.

Strike out if the Master is not a Limited Company.
The Common Seal of _____

_____ , Limited,

was hereunto affixed in the presence of _____

_____

_____

Strike out if the Master is a Limited Company.
Signed sealed and delivered by the above-named

William Rawlinson

in the presence of *W. Hollingshead*
20 Wood Street,
Bolton.

William Rawlinson **(The Master)**

Signed sealed and delivered by the above-named

Frank Dibnah

in the presence of *W. Hollingshead*
20 Wood St. eet,
Bolton.

Frank Dibnah **(The Parent or Guardian)**

Signed sealed and delivered by the above-named

Frederick Dibnah

in the presence of *W. Hollingshead*
20 Wood Street
Bolton.

Frederick Dibnah **(The Apprentice)**

Signed sealed and delivered by the above-named

Arthur Wallwork Talbot

in the presence of *W. Hollingshead*
20 Wood Street
Bolton.

A. Talbot **(The Representative)**

Endorsement of Deed of Apprenticeship

A. We (i) the Master and (ii) the Representative hereby certify that this Deed of Apprenticeship terminated on the ___28th April 1959.___ has been faithfully complied with and is hereby endorsed in accordance with the provisions of Clause 2(k) thereof.

(i) *William Rawlinson* ___Master.___

(ii) *J. F. Bolton* ___Representative.___

B. We further certify that during the period of apprenticeship the Apprentice _____

_____ has attained the following awards: —

(i) _____

(ii) _____

(iii) _____

(iv) _____

At the age of 16 Fred Dibnah took up his apprenticeship as a joiner with Bill Rawlinson. Pictured is a copy of Fred's original papers which were signed in the presence of his father Frank on 4th October 1954.

The Worlds Largest Steam Rally

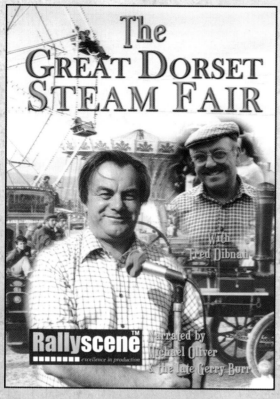

The Great Dorset Steam Fair.
See More Fred Dibnah on this DVD

More Fred Dibnah on this DVD.
NOW ONLY
£12.95
PLUS £2.50 U.K.
POSTAGE & PACKING

This unique video covers the history of the world`s largest steam fair. From it`s humble beginnings to a massive event that it is today.

During the making of this DVD, Paul Donoghue has called upon a huge resouce of material . There are many previous unseen photographs, rare cine films and great interviews with people who have ben with The Great Dorset Steam Fair since the early days. The main commentary is taken up by Michael Oliver along with comments and vies from the late Gerry Burr.

Comments from the late Fred Dibnah, John Wharton and the late Jack Wharton, Richard Preston and the Late Chris Edmonds Jim Sarney and Roger Burville.

The DVD contains special features:
Prestons of Potto - Jim Sarney`s "The Story of Sad Sam"
RUNNING TIME 90 minutes

I loaded up the trailer one winter morning and he set off on his own for Ashton-under-Lyne. Normally he were back about half five yet, when I locked up after six, Mr. Rawlinson had not yet returned. The Wolsley was there next morning but no trailer. Mr. Rawlinson told me he had been zooming up the road from Bolton to Bury when one of the wheels sort of finally gave up the ghost. The rim with the tyre on had gone past him while the trailer with its load ran on to the grass verge and collapsed. "I never did get to Ashton-under-Lyne," Mr. Rawlinson told me. "What now?" I asked. "Oh, I tried to get two new wheels from a scrap man," he replied, "but a quid was too much. Fortunately I've found another axle with wheels on it. Bit of a complicated job though I'm sure you'll manage." Which I did. I had been with him the longest, though every now and then he would sign on somebody if we were a bit busy to help me out of the muck like.

The rim with the tyre on had gone past him while the trailer with its load ran on to the grass verge and collapsed.

Fred smartly dressed after securing his joinery apprenticeship.

One day a peculiar fellow came along. He were a strange sort of man who smoked a briar wood pipe and wore a long black overcoat.

"I want you," Mr. Rawlinson told me, "to keep an eye on that fellow. He likes having a drink, y'know." 'Nothing unusual about that,' I thought, but said nothing. There were a hand cart in the yard for local jobs almost as knackered as the trailer.

Fred Dibnah at work putting his art skills into practice.

The new man and I had to load it with two lengths of guttering, two ladders and our tool bags. We were about half way up a hill when the new fellow takes a hammer out of his bag and proceeds to smash one of the wheels. Of course, the cart falls over with me left looking at it. The fellow went to the nearest phone box, rang Mr. Rawlinson and said the old cart had collapsed. This meant the gaffer coming out in his car and trailer. Mr Rawlinson did not seem too surprised about the hand cart and I kept my mouth shut.

I continued to keep my mouth shut about the new fellow who did have a drink problem. Early each afternoon he would say to me, "Just going for a box of matches." It always took him an hour or two to get them. Once, I was alone on some roof when I heard the ladder shaking and clattering. It were the new fellow and he was properly topped up with ale. In the end I had to send for Mr. Rawlinson to help get him down to the ground. And that were the end of him as well.

Mr. Rawlinson had yet another man come to work for us. One day this new fellow and I were proceeding somewhere when we saw an enormous chimney out in the country. It was 262ft tall, had red ladders stuck up the side and staging round the top. Those staging planks were 22ft long yet they looked like matchsticks.

"I'd love to climb up there," I said. 'You'd never do it," said this fellow. So I laid him a wager of ten bob that I would not only get to the top but also leave proof of my climb.

The next job we had were at a park site. In the park keeper's hut I found a large Union Jack about 8ft tall and 14ft long. Without saying anything I rolled up the flag and shoved it inside my jacket. It made a bit of a bulge. On my way home a young roof slater I knew asked what it were I was hiding in my jacket, like. "It's a Union Jack," I said. "I'm going to climb that chimney back there and fly the flag from one of the two lightning conductors, for a bet." "Better still," said the roof slater, "I've got another Union Jack at home. I'll give you mine as well." You see, he were as mad as me.

Now the chimney was situated a long way from the works with its flue running underground through a wood. There were also a bit of a stone wall round the base to keep out foolhardy people. So I had to do the job at night. On arriving at the stack I found they had taken away the first 16ft ladder. I tied an old nut to a piece of string and threw it over the bottom rung of the second ladder. Using the string, I pulled a rope through and then proceeded to climb the main stack.

Students were blamed for the hanging of the dummy, but Fred won his bet with ease.

Fred Dibnah steeplejacking on his mind as he prepares for a big stunt.

On reaching the top I tied the two union jacks to the lightning conductors, came down and went home rather sooty state. Of course, there were a lot of "Where have you been?" and all that, but I did not let on to me parents.

Next day in the local evening paper, there was a magnificent picture of the chimney with the two union jacks fluttering from the top. For some unknown reason the authorities blamed it on the Manchester University students who were having their rag week at the time. I had quite a job collecting my ten bob until this roof slater fellow backed me up about the second flag.

We then came up with the idea of a tailor's dummy to look like a man hanging from the top of another chimney. Mr. Rawlinson always went home for his dinner, so I started constructing the fake corpse out of wood lathes and fencing wire. It were basically one straight stick for the backbone and a stick the other way for the arms. Coiled wire made the torso, then there were a bit of board for the pelvis with legs dangling downwards.

I made the head from a sack filled with old rags. Next we had to dress the dummy, which called for all our ingenuity. My mate's wife were always going to jumble sales and she had bought him a monstrous overcoat which he did not like. I supplied some old pants and a pair of me father's boots filled with concrete to make the hanging man look right. The body folded over at the shoulders so I could tie the whole thing together and fit it in a haversack.

The chimney I selected was 212ft tall and was situated on a road near the town centre. John Faulkner's men were working on this chimney with their red ladders all in position. Although we went there at night, all the factory lights were still on and the boilers going at full blast. Me mate took me as near as possible to the place, but it still meant negotiating about 24 back gardens before getting to where I wanted to be. The climb up the stack were no trouble. Soon them lights were twinkling away far below me before they sort of faded. It were pitch black when I reached the staging and as I started to untie the dummy, the wind got inside it. How it ended up was quite unbelievable. Its legs were still over the shoulders while the rope for hanging it came under the crutch. Worse still the whole thing spun like a propeller. I thought to myself, 'This isn't going to be a success' and tried to drag it back again, fighting against the wind at 212ft. But it were no good. The dummy was being blown outwards at forty five degrees, and for a man supposed to be hanging himself it looked horrible. So I just came down that chimney, bought myself some fish and chips and went home.

The next day was a foggy Saturday with no wind. As bad luck would have it, I were working on the other side of town. I could hardly wait for 12 o' clock. The moment it was knocking off time I set off for the chimney, sort of like the crow flies.

"Some silly sod," this fellow replied
"hung a dummy from the top of that chimney."

I went through gardens, across a cemetery and along the Bolton to Blackpool railway line. When I reached the chimney area there was no sign of the hanging dummy, but groups of people stood at street corners as though there had been some sort of disaster. I said to a couple of women and a fellow, "What's going on like?" "Some silly sod," this fellow replied, "hung a dummy from the top of that chimney." "Go away," I said. "What happened?" Then the women started telling me all together at the same time. It seems that an old boy who lived on the main road across the mill woke up at first light, looked out of the window and saw the dreadful spectacle. Soon the whole neighbourhood was up and about with one person after another ringing up the police, the fire brigade and ambulances. "The mill manager was dragged out of bed," one of the women kept saying in a knowing way. "Dragged out of bed." "Then they dragged John Faulkner's foreman out of bed," said the other. "They knocked him up then got him down here. The police told him he would have to climb the chimney and retrieve the dead body."

Shortly afterwards, I learned, someone arrived with a pair of binoculars and those in the know realised it were a practical joke.

Nevertheless John Faulkner's foreman had to bring down the dummy for analysis like. In the pocket of the jumble sale overcoat they found a Manchester bus ticket and the university students again got the blame. The story did not quite end there. Sometime later Mr. Rawlinson had me fitting a new floor in a semi near to the self-same chimney. The lady of the house was very talkative, so I asked her weren't that the stack from which the Manchester students hung a dummy? To my amazement, she broke into a hell of a frenzy. "It may have been a dummy," she said all fierce like, "but my husband didn't know that and had a heart attack." "A heart attack," I gulped. "Fortunately he got over it," she continued to my relief, "but it were a bad sort of thing." "Yes, it were," I agreed, feeling relieved.

"It may have been a dummy," she said all fierce like, "but my husband didn't know that and had a heart attack."

I am still a one for practical jokes, yet I never did anything like that again. Also it made me think. There I were turned 20 doing the same old joinery and gable ends for Mr. Rawlinson. True, he let me call him Bill, and I were his senior man so to speak, but I was neither a steeplejack nor my own gaffer. Whenever I spoke of this to me dad he would say, "You're still young, Fred. Something'll turn up."

Fred Dibnah the good looking young man from Bolton wanted to be his own boss. He was desperate to start working for himself as a steeplejack.

Fred being filmed by the BBC as he prepares to put
a weather cock on the top of a church spire.

"It's a funny thing this celebrity. If you don't wave back you're a miserable bugger, if you do wave back you're a big-headed bugger. I don't know."

The Gypsy Collection

A Gypsy Gathering at Appleby Horse Fair.

Everyone is welcome at Appleby Fair. It is one of those rare events where there is no admission fee. You are an invited guest, where you can watch gypsies washing there horses in the River Eden, find horse dealers buying and selling Skewbald and Piebald ponies, see sulkies racing down the lane to Long Marton, or amble along the aisles of the huge market. All the Gypsies in England come to Appleby Horse Fair and bring the sleepy Cumbrian town to life.

If you ever go to Appleby Horse Fair, you will be an invited guest. It's like the aristocracy, the gypsies will be so nice to you, they will treat you with exceptional manners, but you will never be one of them. And as long as you both realise that, you will get along champion.

Features all the action from Appleby Horse Fair, including; living waggons on the road, horse washing in the River Eden, sulky racing on the road to Long Marton, plus very rare film (unseen) footage from Appleby Fair from 1974. **RUNNING TIME 65 minutes approx.**

NOW ONLY
£12.95
PLUS £2.50 U.K.
POSTAGE & PACKING

The Young
Steeplejack

Shortly after, something did turn up. One day I found a fair sized ladder floating in our local river, which were more of an open sewer. Anyway, I fished it out, scraped it clean and painted it bright red. After pointing people's houses all day for Bill Rawlinson, I would point other people's houses in the evenings for myself. Eventually I earned £90 and bought five good ladders.

Following that it were a case of 'acquiring' pulleys and ropes. By acquiring, I mean acquiring. There was an abundance of pulley wheels left lying about in half dismantled mills. As for ropes, the best source was behind Burnley Park football ground where there stood a railway goods yard and a great bridge. Kids used to

take ropes from the yard to make swings under the bridge, so at nights I would acquire their swing ropes while they slept. Lovely ropes they were with green strands running through them, proving they had come from railway company.

Around this time Bill landed a job for me at a big working mill. It meant putting in a baling press and I had the run of the place. That mill had six floors, as well as a tower crying out to be re-pointed. One day when talking to the chief engineer I said casually like, "Your tower needs re-pointing." "Aye," he agreed. "I hear you do a bit of that. How much would you charge?" I said I would want £140, which looking back on it, were ridiculous. It would be more like £2,000 now (based on 1980s prices). Anyway, I then had to explain about only working weekends. Luckily he accepted that and I used every spare minute of my own time re-pointing the mill tower. It was huge, though at least I could get to top through inside stairs then through a trap door.

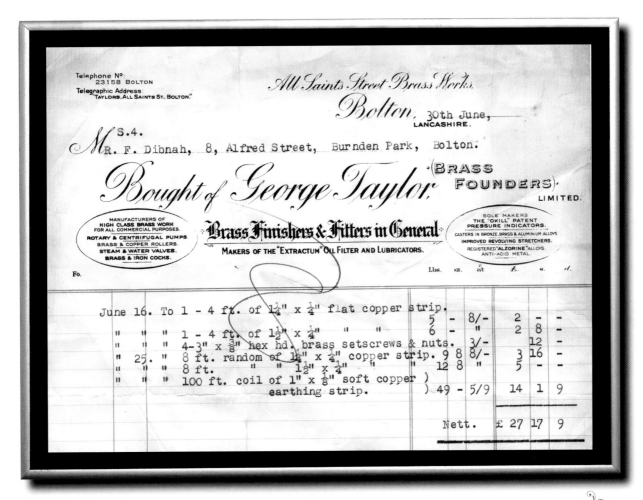

An early photograph of Fred in his work clothes and mucky face.
Caught off guard by an unknown photographer.

By then my employer Bill Rawlinson sort of realised there were more to my interest in steeplejacking than he had at first thought. In those days the fatality rate among steeplejacks were pretty high. Therefore whenever one fell off a chimney it was always mentioned in the newspapers. So Bill would cut out the article and pin it on our workshop door. Soon the door was covered with pictures and details of dead steeplejacks. He used to say it would happen to me but I am still here and he's gone.

However, the job pointing the mill did not solve anything so far as I was concerned. I still did not know how to put ladders up a chimney. I tried talking to John Faulkner's men but they were not very bright. Most had started as labourers doing what they were told. They sort of learned to tie clove hitches, then to pull ladders and planks up chimneys. It were all very vague.

My breakthrough came when I met a man who had been a draughtsman. He had only come into steeplejacking to help his father-in-law who were a bit stuck at the time. This man explained it all to me in very simple drawing terms, on the cobbles of a mill yard. He showed me how I could get myself up a 200ft chimney without actually killing myself.

Almost moonlighting. Fred spending Monday to Friday working for Bill Rawlinson and the weekends steeplejacking.

But there were yet another problem. Although I had some fancy cards printed saying 'F. Dibnah, Steeplejack', whenever I went into those factory front offices, people looked on me as some sort of little lad. To tell the truth, I hardly got anywhere. The only chimney jobs I could find were painting those tin things on the back of dry cleaners' shops. They were insults really, being only about 30ft tall.

Still, I had my eye on something very special. There was a stack to be demolished on a particularly nasty site which the other steeplejacks avoided. It were right to one side of the main line from Bolton to Manchester. The signal box lay just below it and in those days signals were operated by thousands of steel wires running over millions of cast iron wheels. Horrible for the steeplejack, and if you made one mistake it could put the whole railway system out of action. I was determined to do the job, but found it hard to sell myself.

Then I had a breakthrough. I happened to bump into the man who had tried to teach me art at school.

One of Fred Dibnah's early attempts at laddering a chimney.

Fred Dibnah had no fear of hard work. He wanted to be a steeplejack and was amassing the tools of his trade at an early stage.

He had a big Jaguar car and talked posh, but did not have much money. I told him about my steeplejacking ambitions and being held up because I never could get past the front offices of factories. He and I struck a deal there and then. For every job he got me, I would pay him £10. I also told him about the horrible railway chimney job.

With his skills, he got the job for me. Also everything went well. Up went the ladders, no problems there. I put the staging round the top, again no problem. After that I chopped a hole in the bottom of the chimney and proceeded to demolish it – brick by brick. So I earned £100 the hard way and my old art teacher got his £10 as agreed.

Eventually, after a few more successful jobs, I were able to get the jobs myself. One job came my way when I were in the local temperance bar run by me Uncle Fred. He used to brew a concoction called 'Hot Bitters' which, before the main pubs opened on a Sunday, attracted all the hard drinkers. You see, it sort of warmed them up for the other stuff. I would go to this bar all blackened like to show I had been doing something worthwhile. In there were one chap who was a cut above the rest of us. To start with he

wore a clean suit. He also had an easy-going manner. "Hello Fred," he said to me one Sunday morning. "Been working?" "Aye," I said. Then by way of further conversation, I pointed my mug at a chimney we could see from the window of Uncle Fred's temperance bar. It were in poor shape with its lightning conductor leaning over at a drunken angle. I said, "It could do with mending and re-pointing." "Why don't you go and see them?" this chap asked. "It's all too posh in that mill." I sort of explained. "Full of walnut panelling and brass hand rails round the desks." Then this chap in the clean suit said, "Happens I know Mr. Farnwood the owner of the mill. I'll have a word with him for you." The next Sunday morning we were again drinking in Uncle Fred's temperance bar and the chap with the suit came up to me. "I've seen Mr. Farnwood," he said, "and he'd like you to go to mill with a drawing of what should be done."

Everything went well. Up went the ladders, no problems there. I put the staging round the top, again no problem. After that I chopped a hole in the bottom of the chimney and proceeded to demolish it.

Having sort of been to art school, the drawings were no problem. I did an impressive drawing of how a lightning conductor should be fixed to the chimney. There were plenty of details, all coloured as well. The main thing was it impressed Mr. Farnwood. "Right," he said, "you can have the job. If you do a good job, I will pay you. If you make a mess of it, you don't get paid." "Fair enough," I said and meant it.

> *If you do a good job, I will pay you. If you make a mess of it, you don't get paid." "Fair enough," I said and meant it.*

So I had a right important job at last. Up went my red painted ladders. Up went the staging round the top. I mended the lightning conductor, also re-pointed right round some 5ft of the brickwork. Mr. Farnwood said it were all right and paid me. He also had me repairing the roof of his factory.

Now my ladders were fine but the planks I used came from the building trade. This meant they were too short and narrow. As luck would have it I found some longer and wider planks on the factory roof where they were used to cross the weaving shed windows called 'northern lights'. There were so many of these good planks I sort of did a swap. Weeks later I got a letter from Mr. Farnwood himself. Would I come to his mill immediately? 'This is it,' I thought. 'He's missed the planks I nicked.' When I got there Mr. Farnwood took me to one side then remarked,

"See that other chimney up there with the fellow on it?" "Yes sir," I said guardedly like. "Well I don't really like what he is telling me. I want you to go up, inspect the job and give me your opinion. As if you were my consultant." I thought it were a bit unethical but, because of those planks I did as asked.

The job was a big one and in the end Mr Farnwood had me doing it with this other fellow as my assistant. I made good money on that stack, instead of being handed over to the police.

With the money from Mr Farnwood for my unexpected job, I bought yet more ladders. Seeing as how my parents backyard were only 14ft square it was getting a bit full of red ladders. They also stood halfway up the side of the house. Me father began to get a bit uptight about this perhaps because me Mum could not see out of the windows. Fortunately he knew a decorator chap across the street who had a yard and we did a deal. The decorator was looking for someone to do up his premises while I wanted somewhere to put my ladders and other tackle.

Smartly dressed, Fred at the back of the family terraced house on Alfred Street, Bolton.

These premises were in a deplorable state of decay. The wooden fence at the front was falling down and you had to lift the gates to move them. As for the sheds, they were made out of railway sleepers and bits of old timber. I built a new brick wall along the front, re-swung the gates and sorted out everything inside for my ladders, planks, ropes, pulleys, hooks and brackets.

By that time I were both busy and beginning to make money. During the day I still worked for Bill Rawlinson. During the evenings and weekends I worked for myself. The name Fred Dibnah began to be known where tough jobs were needed, particularly high up like. I began to see and plan ahead then the army caught up with me. You see I were 22 years old and should have started my national service at 21. Bill Rawlinson tried to argue the toss on my behalf, saying I were far too valuable to go into the army. The selection board thought about this conferred then said to Bill as if I were not there. We are very sorry Mr. Rawlinson, but you will have to get another operative in place of Mr. Dibnah. You see, the country is a bit hard up for men at the moment. Especially men with skills. He'll have to go."

First I had to go for a medical examination where they felt various parts of me anatomy. After that I went to some sort of careers fellow. I told him all I had done before pleading, "Please give me a job outside like building, engineering or something of that style. If you can keep me in the open air, I'll do my National Service with pleasure. "Great," he said, "because you are going to be in a cookhouse." So I was in the army, like it or not but that is another story...

"If you can keep me in the open air, I'll do my national service with pleasure." "Great, because you are going to be in a cookhouse."

Fred's Mother Betsy visiting Fred's new yard, no doubt happy that she could now see through her windows back at home on Alfred Street.

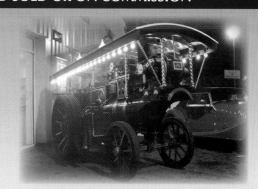

Fred lined up with the rest of his recruits in Aldershot, 1960. Fred is on the bottom row, circled.

Fred Dibnah's National Service

Once he had been pronounced fit, Fred Dibnah had to endure the usual six weeks square bashing at Aldershot. On completing this, he was given the choice of two jobs. Medical Corps or Catering Corps. This upset Fred as he had always worked outside in the fresh air. He pleaded with the sergeant to give him a job repairing tanks or something more appropriate to his skills. His protests fell on deaf ears and he was assigned to the Catering Corps and transferred to Catterick barracks to learn the basic art of cooking. Within six weeks Fred had managed to wangle his way out of the cookhouse and was sent to Germany with the tank regiment The 14/20th

Kings Hussars. He spent his time there working with their horses and hounds. The regiment was situated on a dilapidated farmhouse on the outskirts of the camp, and because of his skill base Fred asked his commanding officers Captain Vivian Jasper Tubbs and Major Faro-Tomlin if he could repair the high pitched roof where the horses were kept and make some brick stables. Permission was granted and as a result Fred Dibnah finished up having a fairly easy National Service. Having done his duty for two years, Fred returned to Bolton, civilian life and his passion, steeplejacking.

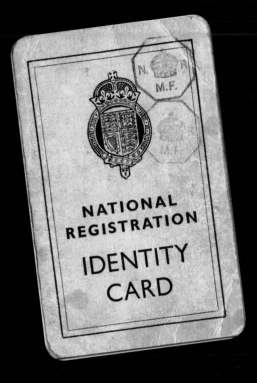

Fred Dibnah in uniform as he reluctantly worked his
way through two years of National Service.

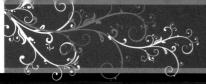

BIG chimneys

MR. F. DIBNAH, whose home address is 8 Alfred-st. (near Bunder Park), writes to us from Germany, where he is at present doing his National Service, asking for some details about chimneys.

Hardly surprising that he should ask about chimneys, for he is a steeplejack in civil life! Mr. Dibnah writes: "Can you tell me something about some old chimneys, such as Dobson's, or the one at Barrow Bridge?"

He also asks did Bolton ever have the biggest chimney in the country. So far as can be traced we never had the country's biggest chimney, but for many years the tallest stack in Lancashire was at Dobson and Barlow's Kay-st. works—367½ft high. For years people argued that it's height was 369½ft. Then Joe Smith, a local steeplejack, climbed up with a tape-measure! After hours of patient measuring he came to earth to announce that the height was exactly 367½ft—and that was that!

Barrow Bridge chimney was formerly 306ft in height, but in 1929 it was reduced to 288ft. Then in 1945 a crack appeared in the fabric so another 36ft. was taken off, making the chimney a mere 252ft.

While serving in Germany, Fred wrote to a local newspaper back home. This was Fred's first newspaper article.

The Gypsy Collection

Appleby Horse Fair - The Golden Year.

In this DVD you will witness the town coming alive with the hustle and bustle of gypsies, horses, dealers and tourists all gathered for the selling and racing of horses that is the mainstay of the fair. You will see the sights and sounds of the fair that has a reputation world-wide, attracting visitors and travellers from all over the globe. Watch the horses being prepared and washed in the River Eden, and see an award winning farrier at work. Meet some of the colourful characters who are regulars to the fair, including a special tribute to the late Johnny Eagle.

RUNNING TIME 65 minutes approx.

Now - £12.95
Plus £2.50 U.K.
Postage & Packing

The Gypsies & Horse Dealers at Appleby Horse Fair.

The month of June comes and goes every year, and for gypsies and horse dealers the month of June is everything. It's the only month in the year when the famous Appleby Fair takes place. This video gives you a unique insight of the fair from the comfort of your armchair. From living waggons on the road, to beautiful Piebold and Skewbold horses in the River Eden, there's singing in the pub and trotting horses in the lanes. Deals, wheels, carts and laughter. This is Appleby Horse Fair, once seen, never forgotten.

RUNNING TIME 55 minutes approx.

Now - £12.95
Plus £2.50 U.K.
Postage & Packing

"A Romany Summer" plus "A Family Affair".

In the early 1970's the late Barry Cockcroft made a series of films called "Once in a Lifetime". These programmes were shown on the whole ITV network. One of the more memorable programmes was called "A Romany Summer", which featured a family of Romany Gypsies who travelled and lived on the lanes around York.
This DVD also shows the gypsies at the popular Lee Gap Fair.

RUNNING TIME 50 minutes approx.

Now - £12.95
Plus £2.50 U.K.
Postage & Packing

Ballinasloe "The Great Horse Fair".

The Ballinasloe October Horse Fair is famous the world over. It is a place to visit if you want to see the best of Irish bloodstock, and that means the best you will find anywhere in the world. The Great Fair brings to life a unique event. For a few days each year, a quiet County Galway town becomes a maelstrom of wheeling and dealing, of bustle and throng, of songs and stories, as more than three hundred years of tradition and a thousand years of history meet head-on in Europe's greatest frenzy of horse dealing. Narrated by respected horseman Graham Schofield.

RUNNING TIME 55 minutes approx

Now £12.95
Plus £2.50 U.K.
Postage & Packing

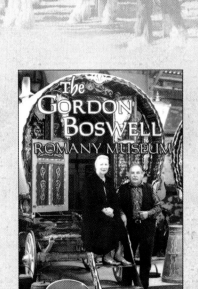

The Gorden Boswell Romany Museum
The Gentleman Gypsy

The Gordon Boswell Romany Museum is a great experience for all the family, containing one of the countries finest collections of Gypsy Caravans, carts and harnesses in the world.

In this unique film, Gordon Boswell talks about the old Romany way of life (as he guides you through all sections of his museum), his ancestors, and how he came to own one of the most beautiful collections of Gypsy tackle.

RUNNING TIME 1 hour 20 minutes approx.

NOW ONLY
£12.95
PLUS £2.50 U.K.
POSTAGE & PACKING

Once my two years was up, I 'escaped' from the army. The great day came when I got on that plane which took me straight back from Germany to Manchester. I drank a bit for the first day or two after reaching home, then I went across to check my steeplejacking things in the decorator's yard. The red ladders were outside, but they had been covered up and no harm came to them. The rest were in a bit of a shed, all ready to be used. So I had cards and bill heads printed, also some photographs of jobs I had done. I was older, more experienced and able to speak for myself. I put on my best suit with a gold watch chain and set off round the mills of Bolton. Some of the chimneys looked right ropey so I was sure to find jobs. In reality, tough times lay ahead.

I was older, more experienced and able to speak for myself. I put on my best suit with a gold watch chain and set off round the mills of Bolton.

Hanging on the walls: a collection of tools for the many different tasks a steeplejack has to perform. Much of the metalwork was prepared in Fred's workshop.

Fred painting a workshop sign by hand.

Rare photograph of Fred Dibnah's first workshop.

A work of art carried out at 200ft above ground level.

*fancy London types
'now the pleasure of
chips with fingers "*

"We've become a nation of con men, living by selling double glazing to each other."

Fred Dibnah
High Climbs

Fred working high up on a miserable Lancashire morning in the damp and cold.

While I were away feeding the troops, things had gone from bad to worse in Bolton. Some of the mills shut down and the others struggled for survival. Their buildings and especially the chimneys needed repairing but there was little or no money available. I found this out the hard way. To begin with, I did not think it best to ride a motor bike round the mills of Bolton wearing my best suit, gold watch and chain. So I used public transport which restricted me to less calls per day. Then, when I got there, they would keep me sitting in the foyer for an hour or more before telling me my services were not required.

Nowadays, I go straight into the managing director or chief engineer, but I have never forgotten those unhappy days of having to wait for nothing. In fact, I had some right rebuffs when I came out of the army and was looking for steeplejack work. After several weeks it began to seem as if I were getting nowhere fast. So for two or three days at a time, I would do odd jobs for local property repairers. You know, a slate on here for Mr. Smith and a new bit of guttering for Mrs. Brown.

Out of the money earned this way, I would give me mum a regular sum for supporting me while the rest generally went on fags and the odd pint. This went on for over six months. Always, after three days repairing, I would go round the mills again for a couple of days. I was after real chimney work but during that time I never got a single stack to mend.

At long last I had a slight stroke of luck. There were three breweries in Bolton, one of them near the art school. The owner's house was next door and I had been quite friendly with his son when we were lads. By now the son had become a man and he worked in the family brewery whose chimney were in a diabolical condition. Partly because of our old acquaintanceship but mostly because something had to be done about that stack before it fell down, I was given the job. I shall never forget the first chimney I ever mended. I spent three weeks making everything perfect for which I earned £45. While doing so, I did not know where the next job was coming from.

View from the top of a mill chimney.

Fred half way up a chimney swinging on his bosun's chair.

Anyway, the brewery stack needed a new metal band round the top and me father introduced me to a welder-cum-metalwork fellow. I talked to this chap quite a bit as he was making the band which fitted fine. After finishing the brewery job, I began searching for more work and thought I would look in to see the welder fellow.

I'm glad you called," he said. "The vicar of Bolton wants to see you." "What for?" I asked.
"Best go and talk to him yourself," he replied. Here I should say a little about that vicar who was a funny sort of fellow. He was a good Christian mind, which can be strange to some clergymen but he had a mad look about him. At that time he drove a huge black 1929 Humber limousine with a bonnet about 6ft long. Anyway, I zoomed off to see him on me 1927 AJS, which he thought were marvellous, so I used it more and more after that.

"Ah yes," he said at last when I managed to bring up the matter of work, "I want you to take a squint at my weathervane." We then both looked upwards as if to Heaven.

If you have ever been to Bolton, you will know that the church tower is the tallest thing in town. From the ground the vane looks like a postage stamp. Actually the main bit is 6ft 6in long and 3ft deep - as big as a back door and made of heavy metal. How them Victorians manhandled it up there in the first place I shall never know. It were going to be bad enough job just repairing it.

To begin with, the task seemed impossible. Fortunately I was able to get most of the way up the tower by a staircase in the middle. This came out level with four pinnacles and from there I had to stick up me red ladders then put scaffold round them. The view from the top was fantastic. It seemed more like 10 miles high than 200ft.

After I had seen to the weathervane, the vicar wanted it gilded all over. This meant putting on gold leaf, not the easiest of jobs at that height on a windy day. I did what was required and, apart from getting my picture in the local rag, which did me a bit of good, this chief vicar chap put a word round the other Bolton clergy.

As I said, he was a bit of a character. Among his many interests he liked firearms. He and I used to sit in the cemetery with him telling me about all the lethal weapons he possessed. Once, when I could get a word in, I mentioned that I had sort of come back from Germany with a Luger pistol. Immediately the mad look came into his eyes. He had to have one, preferably mine.

Among his many interests he liked firearms. He and I used to sit in the cemetery with him telling me about all the lethal weapons he possessed.

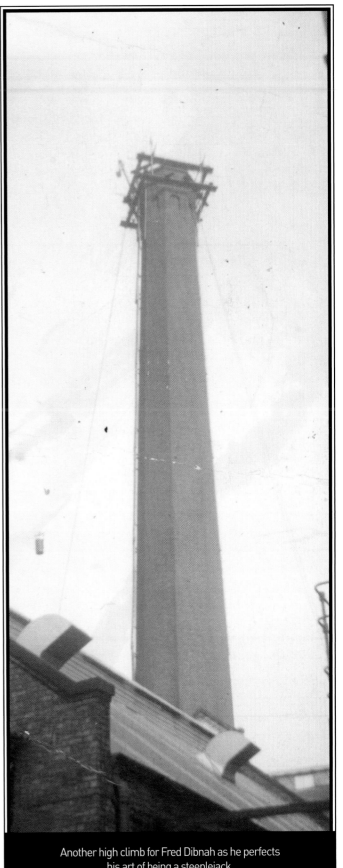

Another high climb for Fred Dibnah as he perfects his art of being a steeplejack.

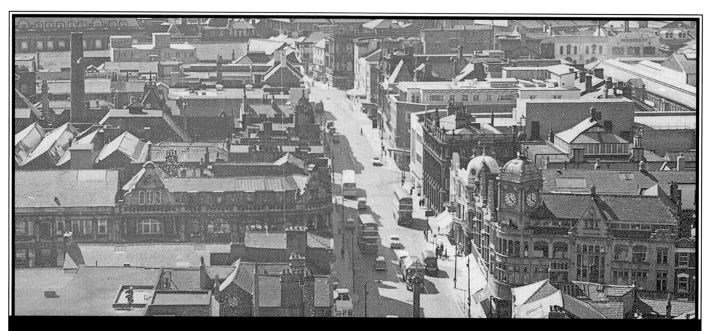

View from Bolton Parish Church looking at the town from above.

I thought it would blow over but the next time we met in the graveyard, the vicar revealed to me he had his own firing range up on the moors. "Whenever I feel like a shootout," he said with that look of his, "I will pack the Humber with my whole armoury in proper Al Capone style." I doubt if he had firearm certificates for half his guns, not bothering much about paperwork as he told me. So I hoped the subject would be dropped. However, the third time we happened to meet in the cemetery the vicar said excitedly, "I'm going up on the moors next Wednesday to have a good blaze away. Care to join me? You could bring that Luger with you."

He would not take no for an answer and it seemed the solution to another problem. You see, me mum did not like the gun – any gun – and she had locked it up in her parlour cupboard. On the Wednesday while she was out at work, the Vicar of Bolton and I arrived outside the house in his black limousine.

Of course I had a key for the front door but we could not find the key for that parlour cupboard. Hunt high and low we did, with him getting wilder as time went on. In the end we had to kind of burgle the cupboard. I was not too keen about it. However the vicar just had to have that Luger.

The story did not end there, though. After we had fired everything on the moors and returned to town, the vicar suddenly remembered another appointment. "Have to visit some parish ladies," he told me. "Would you be a good chap and put my guns in the vestry?"

I had to walk about 200 yards to the church and, as luck would have it, the council just happened to be knocking down the Grand Theatre at the time. All the roads were blocked and there were policemen officiating everywhere. To get to the vestry, I had to talk my way past one policeman after another, pretending I were carrying the tools of me trade. But that vicar was a good friend as I said. He got me my next job mending the clock faces on another church tower. Everything I touched up there came away in my hands and it ended up with some major reconstruction.

"I will pack the Humber with my whole armoury in proper Al Capone style." I doubt if he had firearm certificates for half his guns.

Fred posing for the camera while the chimney in the background is propped up and ready for demolition.

The Parish Church of St. Peter, Bolton
(Bolton Parish Church)

Telephone
FARNWORTH
311

FROM THE HONORARY TREASURER TO THE
PAROCHIAL CHURCH COUNCIL
Mr. JOHN FALLOWS

7, MARKET STREET
LITTLE LEVER
Nr. BOLTON, Lancs.

F. Dibnah Esq.,
8, Alfred Street,
Burnden Park,
BOLTON.

21st October, 1963.

Dear Mr. Dibnah,

what wright Canon Norburn has passed on to me your account, for presentation to the various people who have undertaken to meet different items of the expenses, and for the Fabric Fund Trustees, who will be footing the major portion of the remainder.

You may have some idea of the way that these funds work, but if not, then let me say only that the Trustees will not fork out a penny if they think it is for anything not just in the scope of their own particular Trust Deed. So you have a rough idea of what we are up against.

What I would like you to do, if this can be arranged without great difficulto, is to let me have one account separate, for the gold leaf work on the Weather Vanes.

Then make out another account, ignoring all reference to painting and cleaning down the clock, in such general terms as " repairs to lead work on top, of Church Tower; pointing of four pinnacles in mastic; supplying and fixing new copper lightning conductor strip etc., etc., making good all brackets and iron work and leaving all in good order".

Use your own wording of course, and make sure that the total of this account makes up the balance due to you with the other. You will understand that the Fabric Fund will pay for pretty well anything structural or repair, but not painting and cleaning down.

If you can do this, it will enable the Trustees to sign my cheque with an easy conscience !.

Should you be in any doubt or difficulty, please ring Canon Norburn or myself.

other 105

Yours sincerely,

John Fallows.

Hon. Treasurer to Bolton Parish
Church Parochial Church Council

Official letter from Bolton Parish Church dated 1963.

For example, on top of that church spire there was a huge iron rod, on which the weathervane was mounted, together with a monstrous bolt with a proper head at one end leading through to a nut and washer at the other. If you look up slender church spires and wonder how the weathervane does not blow off, it is because of that rod up the middle, as well as the giant nut, bolt and washer.

Trouble is they were all put up and forgotten over hundred years ago, with the weather helping the rust on ever since. By the time I got there, that bolt was no thicker than a ball point pen. The job sticks in my mind because it were the first of its kind I had to do. I also kept taking photos and putting them in me work album which had 'F. Dibnah Steeplejack' gold embossed on the front.

But mending church steeples was not the same as working on industrial chimneys. So one day I summoned up enough courage to visit the biggest firm in the area, Hick Hargraves. It was a very forbidding sort of place with iron pillars iron door and an iron portcullis type of gate. At 5.30, everyone used to come out of there as if they had been in prison all day.

It was a fine day and I decided to go on my motor bike, which was sort of impressive with carbide lamps and a great bull horn. As luck would have it, I roared into the place and very nearly knocked over the boss man. Fortunately he showed more interest in me bike than the photo album I had strapped on to a back bracket.

Next thing he were saying if I had a moment or two he would take me round his works and show me all the chimneys. It was full of them, most built in the 1860s. I found a big opening there and have had a more or less permanent arrangement with them ever since. The money I made on their first job enabled me to buy 10 more ladders making 30 in all.

Trouble is they were all put up and forgotten over hundred years ago, with the weather helping the rust on ever since.

A typical setup at a chimney top.

Traction Engines
The Great Discovery
50 Year Time Capsule

Only £19.95
+ £3.50 UK P&P

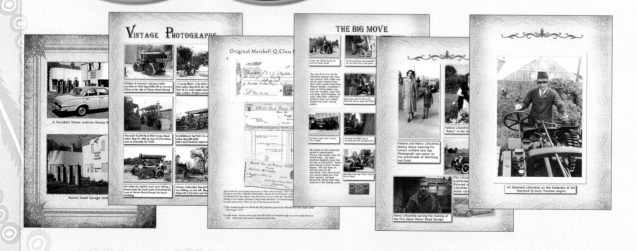

2 FULL LENGTH DVD'S

LIMITED EDITION COLLECTORS PORTFOLIO

Rare Documents & Photographs

The Story of The Lillywhite Traction Engines

There is a garage in East Preston, Sussex, that has kept a secret for nearly 50 years. Six traction engines, numerous vintage cars, and redundant plant, were stored at the Lillywhite Garage with only family and a handful of carefully selected people knowing what lay behind the closed doors.

So important and unique was the find that Heritage film maker Paul Donoghue was asked to scrupulously film the site and preserve the find on film for future generations.

DVD One Steam Traction Engines "The Great Discovery"

This film takes you into the Lillywhite Garage and shows the you the treasures that have laid undisturbed for almost half a century. Presented and narrated by respected steam engineer, Michael Webber, the story unfolds of how an Aladdin's cave of preservation exhibits have waited decades to be discovered.

The highpoint of the film is the unveiling of the extremely rare Marshall 6nhp Q-Class engine. No 73040. This engine was the favourite engine of the garage owner, Mr Reginald Lillywhite, and was stored in a special shed away from the garage.

Packed with rare footage, old photographs, lovely music and great interviews. (running time 60 minutes approx)

am Engineer, **Michael Webber**
the day he unveiled the rare
rshall Q-Class Traction Engine in
ecret building near Manor Road
rage, East Preston, Sussex.

DVD Two Michael Webber`s Sussex Steam Rally

aturing the Lillywhite Engines. With two of the Lillywhite
gines in steam, the other four engines presented as exhibits,
r cameras take you to the beautifully presented Sussex
am Rally. Featuring interviews, working
am, arena events , miniatures, a fairground organ,
del railway and many other great exhibits.

e highlight is seeing the rare Lillywhite Marshall Q-Class
d the Wallace and Steevens Advance Road Roller `in steam
d working after 50 years behind locked doors.
nning time 60 minutes approx)

8 page Limited Edition Document and Photograph
ok accompanies the two DVD`s in this presentation.

Reginald Lillywhite

Buy Now ON-LINE
www.freddibnah.tv

Paul Donoghue Publishing
Office Suite No 7
Station Business Centre
Station Road
Clowne
S43 4RW
Telephone 01246 811112

VISA MasterCard Maestro

SWITCH SOLO

PDP
PAUL DONOGHUE PUBLISHING

We accept all Major Credit Cards: Please make Cheques payable to Paul Donoghue

Now you see it.

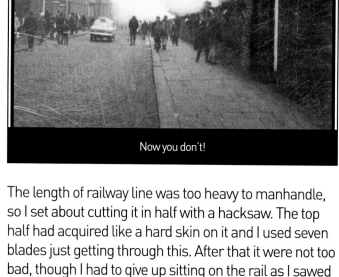

Now you don't!

Up to then I did everything sort of singlehanded, which made the hard work all the harder. So I began to look for an assistant and latched on to an old fellow called Percy Porter. I taught him how to tie knots and handle the equipment then we went out to tackle a 200ft chimney.

Shortly after Percy joined me, I were summoned to an unbelievable chimney 270ft high. I had just enough ladders to go up it, but nowhere near enough scaffolding to go round the top. The engineer told me they wanted the top half of the stack chopped down, as it was surplus to requirements and a liability stuck so far up in the sky. Besides, they had to pay heavy insurance for the thing.

When I reached the top I found a length of railway line the old timers had used. It were like a beam across the centre for pulling up materials. They had moved this beam higher and higher when the chimney was being built. Then, on reaching the top they left it there. Now I had to get it down again.

The length of railway line was too heavy to manhandle, so I set about cutting it in half with a hacksaw. The top half had acquired like a hard skin on it and I used seven blades just getting through this. After that it were not too bad, though I had to give up sitting on the rail as I sawed away towards the end.

There was a bit of spare ground by the foot of the chimney and Percy warned everyone to keep out of the area. The first piece I threw down landed horizontally while the second hit the ground end first. I watched them both disappear into the ground completely, and for all I know are still there.

Anyway, I began taking the chimney down brick by brick Apart from the hard graft this operation was made all the more difficult by the smoke billowing out all the time. You see they could not stop production and, one way or another, it took me six months. Some nights I went home looking like a smoked kipper.

As I bashed away at each brick with my hammer and chisel, I used to think about our ancestors who put up all those mill houses and chimneys. They were sort of building their own pyramids and they did so in style. No one takes much notice of what they did nowadays, but I have had close-up views of all their beautiful stone dressings and magnificent brick formations.

Another bonus was the view one got from the top of a 200ft chimney, especially during the winter. There would be those endless rows of Coronation Street terraced houses, each puffing out smoke to add to that of the big factory stacks. All the smoke would combine to form layers through which the winter sun filtered grey pink in the mornings and deep purple just before nightfall.

In addition to Percy Porter, I took on another man called Joe Robinson. Joe was very strong even when nudging 70 and was of great help to me until he died. I remember one morning, he and me arriving at a stack. There were a real pea soup fog on and we could not see very far up the side. "You're not going up there," said Joe, "to throw things down today?" He said it as if I was a bit crazy. Course I am, I said. "Work must go on. So you rope off a landing area in case any fool walks into the firing line."

Well up there it was like being in an aeroplane above the clouds. The sun was bright and beautiful, which made me kind of carefree. I started slinging bricks off but forgot that while doing this, I were working my way round the chimney stack. Before long, I were well away from the roped off landing area.

Another bonus was the view one got from the top of a 200ft chimney, especially during the winter. There would be those endless rows of Coronation Street terraced houses.

Fred showing off one of his early weathervane designs.

One of the very first colour photographs taken by Fred Dibnah.

Fred's first Land Rover.

It began to dawn on me that when I threw a brick down, a different sort of noise came up through the fog. So I chucked another in the same direction and the sound of breaking slate or glass reached my ears. Next thing there were shouts from below like 'Oy!'. Then I remembered that on the opposite side of the chimney from my landing area for bricks there stood a rather splendid office.

It had a slate roof, plenty of big glass windows and a fancy plastered ceiling. Below that came the walnut panelling and what they called their 'terrazzo hallway'. But I was worried more about killing somebody as I went down the ladders three rungs at a time.

When I reached the ground and looked towards the building it was to see everyone cowering in a doorway. They were all covered in plaster from the owner of the place downwards. No one said a word to me as I wandered into the terrazzo hallway and up to their once magnificent office.

The first sight I came across were some cornice mouldings about a foot thick laying beside the door. Beyond it lay layer upon layer of roof plaster into which some fair-sized chimney bricks stuck out like they had been dropped by dive bombers. The desks, typewriters and even the tea cups had been properly peppered.

Everyone was so relieved to have escaped loss of life or limb, they treated it like some great adventure. I was glad to go along with that and, in the end, had to repair the roof. Years later, I had to remove the rest of the chimney and I wandered into the office to bring back the memory like. The evidence were all there if you knew where to look and the people talked excitedly to me about it as if they had been in the Battle of the Somme.

As I bashed away at each brick with my hammer and chisel, I used to think about our ancestors who put up all those mill houses and chimneys.

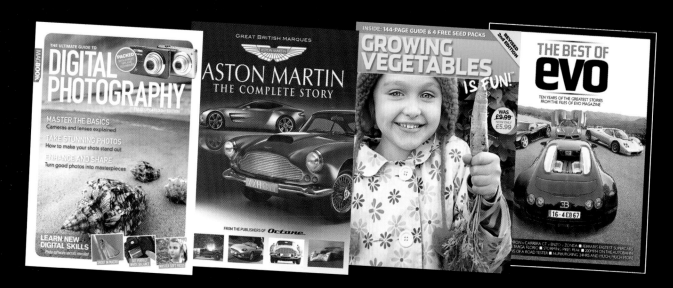

The old way: taking a chimney down brick by brick.

"You're trying to frighten me," the fellow said, "but I'm not at all scared." "Be it on your own head then," I said and meant it. A few days later there was frantic knocking on our front door. Outside was this warehouse fellow who told me he had a problem. "What sort of problem?..." I began to ask when he said, "It's that chimney – bits are beginning to fall off it."

Well I were round there quicker than he was. When I arrived at the warehouse, the place was swarming with police and building inspectors. As usual, when anything falls off a chimney, everyone panics. The fellow was white about the gills yet in a way he were a lucky man.

After that I became very safety conscious, not only for myself but on account of others. I kept a lookout for dangerous chimneys and could spot them a mile off. There was a stack I remember above a warehouse sort of place where I went to buy a replacement cupboard for the one me mum kept complaining had been wrecked in getting the Luger pistol out. An old colliery had originally occupied the site and the chimney stood over the unused engine house.

This stack were in a terrible shape as I noted on entering the yard. So I bought the cupboard all smiles there, then I suggested putting right their chimney. Even when I brought along my photo album, to show I were genuine like, the warehouse fellow was not convinced. "Look." I argued, "that iron ring round the top is hardly holding itself together let alone the chimney. See how those bricks are bulging. There's a lot of pressure behind them. All you need is a change in temperature and bang-crash. It will come down like one of those medieval things them knights used in battle."

Sometimes steeplejacks have to ladder both sides of a chimney as is shown in this early photograph.

When I arrived at the warehouse, the place was swarming with police and building inspectors. As usual, when anything falls off a chimney, everyone panics.

Fred following another successful demolition.

Luckily for him the piece of stack fell away from an adjoining house. If it had come down on the other side of the chimney, the bit would have gone straight through the house both floors. There had been a girl asleep in the top room and people downstairs. As I said, the warehouse fellow were lucky and he had changed his tune completely. "How much will you charge to do it for me?" he asked, then proceeded knocking me down to a rockbottom price.

But the job had to be done and I did it. I took the top 6ft off the chimney, put a new iron band round and pointed 10ft downwards. Finally, just before I was ready to remove my ladders, this warehouse fellow said to me, "I have had some company name signs prepared. I want you to fix them up there, right at the top so everyone can see them." I tried explaining to him that you are not supposed to put up business signs without permission from council but he replied, "If you want me to pay you, you'll do as I say." So I did, with one of his signs facing the town hall. After that I whipped my ladders away. It were not many hours before he phoned me. The town hall had been on to him saying his signs were illegal and must come down immediately. "Right," I told him, "but it will be another job, and I want paying before I put my ladders up." "Right," he agreed between his teeth. He did not want to keep the signs so I used the wood from them to make more kitchen cupboards and placate me mum.

Here I should explain that steeplejacking can be like a bug that bites you. When I was working on the warehouse chimney, a young fellow kept hanging round. We got talking and I could see he was bitten by the bug despite him being a violinist in the Halle Orchestra. He was in the front row so he must have been good. His name was Kenneth.

After the warehouse job, I had to take down a massive 200ft chimney for Courtaulds. It was going to be a big task and, when he heard of it, Kenneth asked if he could assist like. Instead of practising for some concert in the Free Trade Hall, he came and helped me ladder that chimney to the very top and then would sometimes play his violin. I really enjoyed listening to him.

We managed to knock the top 40-50ft off the chimney, then things became difficult. Some bricks were hard and others soft, the same for the mortar, but nothing would break away easily. Those old chimney builders must have known a trick or two that I did not know. Kenneth was as intrigued as me in cracking the job. One of the things we thought of was to take a road drill up there. It were a bit precarious like but we had a go. That did not work either. When we put the bit of the drill into the bricks, it just bored a hole, and yet nothing would come away. Another problem was I had not quoted enough for the job and the weeks were going by.

Big cracks at the top of a chimney. Fred always took photographs so that he could show his clients what needed fixing.

Kenneth the violinist and I thought of everything. We thought of a few 'popper' but Courtaulds did not want explosives. We devised some incredible mechanical contraptions with screw jacks and still that chimney held together. We then used a 50 ton hydraulic jack in another fantastic contraption. After that we worked inside the chimney chiselling away the entire bottom lining.

Then all of a sudden came disaster. The chimney, which had been so stubborn, decided to split right down the middle. One piece about 4ft square went down its centre. Another piece, twice as big bounced off the side and went through the roof of Courtaulds' blacksmith's shops, hitting the main shaft which drove all their machinery. I said to Kenneth the violinist, "At least you have a job with the Halle. My steeplejacking career seems to have come to an end."

While this disaster were taking place, the chief engineer was playing billiards in the canteen at the other end of the works, it being his dinner hour. One of the lads raced across to the canteen like a whippet and broke the news in blunt North of England style. "Fred's just wrecked the blacksmith's shop."

Luckily for me this chief engineer were a Sir Francis Drake type, you know, the one who played bowls while Armada sailed up Channel. "Anyone killed?" he asked still squinting along his cue. "No sir." "Oh well, I'd best finish off this game, then I'll have a look."

That chimney resisted me until the end. Apart from the 50 ton jack, I took a steam roller to it, then pulled off lumps with a wire halter. When it were all over, Kenneth the violinist and I went into a pub and got completely drunk. Maybe it was the drink, but I fancied the ghosts of the Victorian men who had built that stack were laughing at me.

Luckily for me this chief engineer were a Sir Francis Drake type, you know, the one who played bowls while Armada sailed up Channel.

Fred also used a method of jacking up the brickwork to make demolitions easier than using a hammer and chisel all day.

Hard at work with a jackhammer removing the bricks from the chimney that is shown in the beginning of the television series "A Year with Fred".

		£	s.	d.
10/1/63.	Repairs to roof at 142 Radcliffe Rd. 36 new 20" × 10" slates, 30 ft slate lath, 7 sq yards roof felt, sand cement.	12.	o.	o.
12 Jan 1963.	Ce hast, Silencers Bolton limited. Bradly mills lever st little lever.			
ONE.	Demolishing and removeing to lodge	280.	o.	o.
TWO.	Just demolishing. 250.	200.	o.	o.
4 Feb/1963.	Farnworth Cromium plating co Repairs to chimney Pointing with cement and painting iron bands All were necessary 100 120. Top 40 sq yards	185. 47.	o.	o.
11 Feb 1963.	LESLIE FINK estate agents. No 15 Ridgefield, deansgate Manchester. Repairs to chimney at lever st mills 1 new rod. 7 iron bands painting pointing copings Mr Mackenzie.	89.	o.	o.

Demonstration of Fred Dibnah's neat copperplate writing. Taken from his work ledger dated 1963.

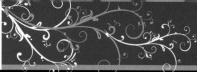

Fred Dibnah

- THE EARLY DAYS -

TELEGRAMS: "INSURANCE, BOLTON" TELEPHONE: BOLTON 26611 (5 LINES)

HINDLEY, KNIGHT & Co. LTD.,
INCORPORATED INSURANCE BROKERS

ESTABLISHED 1899

DIRECTORS
D. HINDLEY, F.C.I.B.
D. HINDLEY, JR. F.C.I.B.

89, Newport Street,

Bolton, 11th February 1963.

F. Dibnah, Esq.,
8, Alfred Street,
Bolton.

Dear Sir,

　　　We are pleased to advise that we have now obtained a rate of premium to include your work as a Steeplejack, and for a limit of indemnity of £25,000 in respect of any one accident the additional premium would amount to £17. 10s.0d annually, which would be subject to adjustment on receipt of the annual wages declaration.

　　　We shall be pleased to discuss this quotation with you at any time convenient to yourself and to arrange the necessary cover on receipt of your instructions.

　　　We are still awaiting quotation for Employers Liability Insurance, and immediately this is received, we shall contact you again.

　　　　　　　Yours faithfully,
　　　　　for HINDLEY, KNIGHT & CO. LTD.,

BM/CAL

F. Dibnah

POLICY

PUBLIC RISK

No. 4442

Amount of Indemnity £25,000.

Renewal Date 24th June.

This Policy should be carefully read by the Insured.

Incorporated Insurance Brokers
89, NEWPORT STREET, BOLTON

Fred Dibnah's early insurance documents. He couldn't pursue the big jobs without insurance.

~ 64 ~

FULLY INSURED

F. DIBNAH
STEEPLEJACK
8 ALFRED STREET, BURNDEN PARK, BOLTON

REPAIRERS OF CHIMNEYS AND CHURCH SPIRES, LIGHTNING CONDUCTORS ERECTED, FLAG POLES PAINTED
AND REPAIRED, CHIMNEYS HOOPED, RAISED AND REPOINTED, IRON CHIMNEYS PAINTED AND REPAIRED

Mr. Howarth   April 24 1963
No. Junction Rd Bolton

			£	s.	d.
No. 14.	No. To,				
	Repairs to gutters, Rain water pipes Chimney stack cement works, and the sweeping of one chimney stack				
6.	6' × 3½" Cast iron RWP,	25s	7.	10.	0.
1.	3½" " " " RWP head,			16.	0.
1.	3½" " " " RWP Offset.		-	16.	0.
2.	6' × 2" Alloy RWP,		1.	6.	8.
1.	2" " " RWP Shoe,				
24.	4" Spout nails,			3.	0.
1.	6' × 3" Asbestos RWP			15.	0.
1.	3" Drive in bracket			3.	0.
1.	17' × 5" × 4" Wooden gutter, per foot 3s 6d	2.	19.	6.	
	Workmans time at 1s per hr 20 hrs.	£7.			
	The sweeping of one chimney stack.		10.	0.	

Dated 24th April 1963. One of Fred's beautifully handwritten invoices.

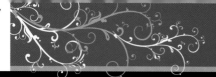

"...nybody who destroys anything ...e of stone should be prosecuted. ...s not all beautiful, but it took a ...an all day to make one stone."

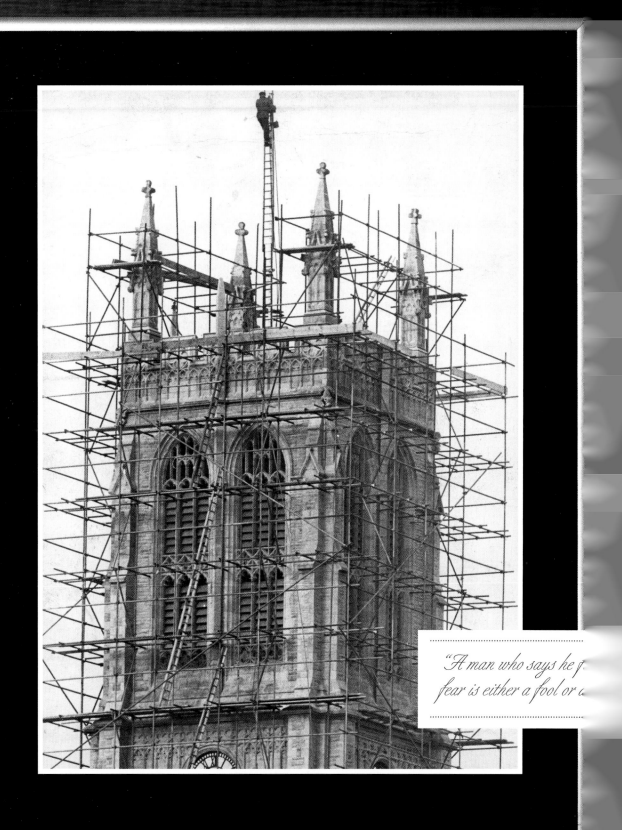

"A man who says he f...
fear is either a fool or ...

Fred Dibnah
Odd Jobs

The nearest I have ever come to death, funny as it may seem, was not up a chimney but down a hole in the ground. An estate agent I knew lived in the country and he had an old well in his garden which worried him. There were two big flagstones over the top, with a crack down the middle and my friend wanted me to find out how deep the well was and if it were dangerous.
I lay squinting between the flagstones, then set fire to pages of the Financial Times and watched them burning until they reached the bottom. This seemed to be 40 or 50 feet down, quite dry and might have been a mineshaft. I made enquiries and learned there were very early types of coal mines in my friend's part of the country. Anyway, I left it at that because the flagstones seemed to be enormous.

However, the estate agent was still worried about such a great hole on his property. To begin with, cars had to drive across these flagstones; also he had a great traction engine which went quite close to the side. One winter's morning, he found where I was working and

came to see me. "Fred," he said, "I must have that well or mineshaft seen to. Repaired or filled in. It's bothering me. Next thing you know there'll be an accident." I said I would do it, little knowing that I would be the victim.

The agreed date arrived. Together with Donald my assistant at the time, we loaded up the van and set out to the estate agent's place. Our first task was to remove those flagstones which proved even harder than I imagined, being about 8ft long by 4ft across and over 3in in thickness. It took time and effort to lift those flags, and then move them out of the way.

Now we could look down the shaft and what we saw proved more peculiar still. For the first 15ft or so, the sides were lined with bricks but not as we know them. These bricks were about 2in thick and had been laid without mortar. After that came rock faces with bits of rotten timber sticking out here and there. All in all, it looked rather dangerous and unhealthy.

One winter's morning he found where I was working and came to see me. "Fred," he said, "I must have that well or mineshaft seen to. Repaired or filled in.

Early photograph of Fred outside his newly built engine shed on Radcliffe Road.

The next thing we did was to put two long scaffolding pipes across the top from which Donald could lower me in my bosun's chair. This preliminary inspection clearly showed that many of the lower bricks were falling away: it seemed to me that we could undermine the bad areas, put a proper footing in the rock face, and then make good the missing bricks. In order to get 15ft down, we suspended four more scaffolding poles from the crosspieces and fitted smaller ones below to hold a working platform. At the beginning, everything went to plan. We repaired one area and then started on another. Then I became inquisitive to see what lay at the bottom of the well, or mineshaft. There might, I thought, be interesting tunnels leading off it. I also thought the bosun's chair would be perfectly safe. It had carried me up and down many a chimney and it would take more than my weight to break the ropes.

One of Fred's early work companions, (the late) Donald Paiton.

You get a feeling about these things. I thought something is seriously wrong and I must get out of here.

A fearless Fred Dibnah, walking around the boards at the top of a Lancashire chimney stack.

So telling Donald what I was doing, I began to lower myself slowly and cautiously. When I was about 3ft from what looked like the bottom, bits and pieces of bricks began to fall around me, some hitting my flat cap. At the same time, Donald's voice echoed down to me. "You'd better come up Fred. Summat seems wrong." By then the lumps were getting bigger and had me worried. Something was really wrong, but I still had no idea of the real danger. Nevertheless I do not think any man ever went up vertically quicker in a bosun's chair than me, right then, in the whole history of bosun's chairs! I was up to the top in record time and Donald quickly pulled me away from that strange hole in the ground.

We waited for a bit, looking this way and that, but nothing more happened. Thinking it were a false alarm, I went back down to the working platform 15ft below the surface. Donald then handed me my brick laying equipment before fetching me a load of bricks. While he was getting them, I decided to knock a bit of broken brick out of the ancient wall. I gave it a preliminary tap like and, all of a sudden, the wall began groaning. You get a feeling about these things. I thought something is seriously wrong and I must get out of here. At the same time I remember thinking that I must also take my trowel and spirit level with me. It is strange how your mind works in a dire emergency. However, I was up and over the top a split second before everything around me started to slide down the hole.

I mean everything. All the old bricks went, the platform I had been standing on was smashed to bits and those extra strong scaffolding poles were bent like paperclips. Even the two pipes across the top were taken some 40-50ft down the shaft before jamming themselves between the rock faces.

The whole episode were a bit of a horror really, but we had not come to the end of it. What I had thought was the bottom had been a piece of wood with debris on it resembling a firm dry surface. The weight of the crashing bricks cleared all that away and it went a further 70ft to black water at the bottom. I am not a swimmer so, if the fall of rocks had not brained me, I would have drowned down there for sure.

You might think Donald and I had had enough. To us, however, that accident was a stroke of luck. The fall of old bricks cleanly cleared away the entire rock faces. We used about 5,000 new bricks in their place, nice and solid all the way round. We then fitted two big iron girders, which could take the weight of a Centurion tank, before putting the flagstones back in position. You would never know they had been moved yet they were as I have related and brought me the nearest I have come to death thus far.

Death and danger are things you have to live with as a steeplejack, you also see them from new angles. This is very noticeable when working on church steeples above graveyards. Many a time I have looked straight down on such places, all empty and desolate. Then more often than you would imagine, a cortege pulls up with the hearse in front and just one car behind.

I always stop working at such times and pay my respects to the departed. Whenever I see just the vicar in front and the widow behind, with not a single friend following, I wonder what the fellow had been like. At other times, I see these little coffins, barely a foot long and 6in wide. They are generally planted across the end of some other grave that nobody knows about. Soon the grass grows over them and both look lonely from where I am watching 200ft above the ground. It's a funny thing is life and death.

I decided to knock a bit of broken brick out of the ancient wall. I gave it a preliminary tap like and, all of a sudden, the wall began groaning. You get a feeling about these things.

Fred lighting the fire on one of his now famous chimney demolitions. His famous quote:
"Once the fire is lit, it's out of your hands; it's in the hands of 'The Man in the Sky'."

Fred taking a deep draw on a cigarette as he ponders where to start removing the bricks from the base of this chimney stack.

Thousands of bricks are removed from the bottom of a chimney stack during Fred Dibnah's unique demolition process.

The first grave I ever dug gave me several problems. There needs to be quite a depth to a grave, say 6ft or more.

Working on churches puts you in touch with all sorts of other people. On one occasion I met a travelling grave digger who had an old car and a stack of new shovels. He told me about his trade and I happened to mention that I was trying to set up a blacksmith's shop but needed an anvil. As luck would have it, the grave digger said he knew of an anvil which had been thrown away about 10 years ago. It turned out that a lot of broken stones had also been thrown over the anvil and it would need digging out. This grave digger said he had hurt his back but, if I could help him dig a few graves, he would in turn help me to recover the anvil. So I ended up being an amateur and part-time grave digger myself.

The first grave I ever dug gave me several problems. There needs to be quite a depth to a grave, say 6ft or more, but by the time you get to 4-5ft down it is difficult to throw out the shovelfuls of clay. They begin to tumble back and you get to thinking about being buried yourself. Trick is to leave a hump in the middle and take it out

last. Anyway, I was digging this grave in what I thought was virgin soil when the shovel struck something hard. That's strange I thought, then the next stroke took the shovel head across the top of a coffin, which could not have been there long because there was a cross on it. At least there was, until my shovel sheared the four screws holding it down and the cross sort of jumped up at me. I froze and looking down saw there were a big crack right along the middle of the coffin lid, which went inwards, and a large knot hole which definitely had space below it. I had not reckoned on a Count Dracula job so I was out of that hole smartish and went to my grave digger friend for advice. "Often happens," he told me, "in this business. You'll have to fill it in again I'm afraid and start somewhere else."

Even when the grave digger's back was better and he had helped me get my anvil, we continued to do mutual business. It worked this way. He would dig the grave and I would fill it in after the funeral ceremony. This meant he could take on more jobs while it was extra cash for me. "Right Fred," he would say, "there's a grave dug in such and such a churchyard and the funeral will be over by 2.30. I'll leave a spare shovel in the boiler house."

I learned that church boiler houses were the favourite place for grave diggers to leave their shovels, also there were other tricks to the trade. For example, grave diggers sometimes cheated on the depth of the holes, but always left the earth looking piled up high with a bit of imitation grass over the top.

Anyway, I would nip down from whatever steeple I were mending in the vicinity. As I said, it brought in a few more quid. However, the rather shallow graves left by my digger began to be criticised by undertakers and I started to get the blame. Not that undertakers were blameless themselves. Theirs was also a peculiar trade. There was one fellow I knew who ran a collection of very large, muscle-bound assistants who swore profusely, and played cards every dinner time and always lost all their wages to him. They would look quiet and humble like on duty but a moment later were drinking and smoking again with great gusto. One day, this head chap said he would show me inside the crematorium, you know, what goes on behind them purple curtains. Up to then, like most other people, I had heard unbelievable tales of coffins not being burnt, then sold again and again to other bereaved relatives. Well that is all rubbish. Basically what happens is this. After the deceased has rolled away to a nice gentle tune on the organ, the coffin with him or her in it, is put on what resembles a huge iron trolley, something like the one used for operations in hospitals. Then the coffin and deceased within are wheeled into the furnace which works off gas and compressed air. It looks like a baker's oven with knobs and dials outside.

This crematorium chap told me that a fragile old lady took about 20 minutes and a 6ft fellow up to an hour. You can look through a spy hole into the furnace while it is going full blast. At first, all one can see is the end of the coffin, then the sides sort of blow out and the top caves in. After that there is just a pile of something burning steadily. At this stage the gas and air would be turned off, the door opened and a big rake shoved inside to break things up a bit, before continuing with the incineration process.

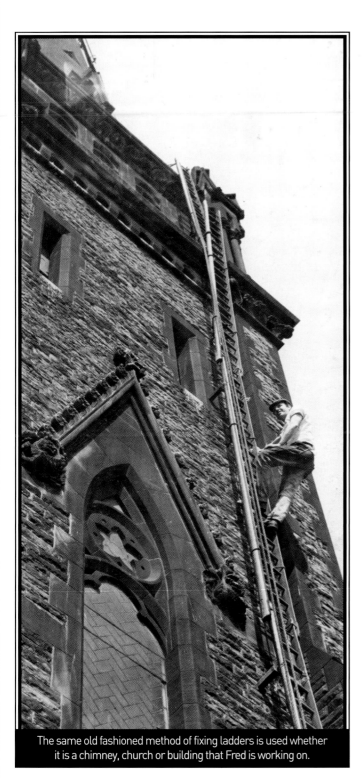

The same old fashioned method of fixing ladders is used whether it is a chimney, church or building that Fred is working on.

This crematorium chap told me that a fragile old lady took about 20 minutes and a 6ft fellow up to an hour.

A mucky Fred on board his prized possession.

Fred's first (ex army) Land Rover in front of a chimney he was working on. Notice the phone number.
Even after Fred became famous you could still phone Bolton 31303 and Fred would answer himself.

Fred's hard working assistant (the late) Donald Paiton posing on a pile of bricks for an entry in one of Fred's many photograph albums.

At the end, after a cooling-off period, what remains is pushed along a little passage at the back. The next stage is to run an electro-magnet over these rough remains so as to extract coffin nails and other interesting pieces of metal like stainless steel hip joints, knee caps and, what was popular at one time, pieces of shrapnel left in peoples bodies following the war.

After the 'de-nailing process' as it is called, comes the final part of reducing the remains to a fine ash. This is done in a grinding machine which looks very much like an old-fashioned gramophone with the horn sticking up at the top. The last mortal remains are tipped into it, and pass through the grinders which are quite powerful as they often have to deal with bits of leg bone, pelvis and the odd skull.

After watching the entire process of reducing a human body to fine ash, I thought the whole thing a bit pathetic and definitely not for me. So when my time comes, I will be buried outside where it is wet and windy.

All this might sound morbid but what I am trying to say is that steeplejacking takes one into some very strange places. I mentioned wet and windy because then you have to come down from the church steeple you are mending and hang around waiting for the weather to improve. You get a lot of time to think. For example, when I am alone in a churchyard, waiting for the rain clouds to blow by, I tend to read the grave stones. Some are very interesting and there is one that particularly sticks in my mind. It is the grave stone of Joseph Spragg, killed during a colliery disaster in 1873. He was buried in the pit, eventually brought out and buried again in a proper cemetery. Somehow I think Joseph would have liked that.

There was another gravestone where the deceased left strict instructions for all his sins to be listed wine, women and dirty songs, the lot. I found that really funny and laughed for days after seeing it.

The next stage is to run an electro-magnet over these rough remains so as to extract coffin nails and other interesting pieces of metal like stainless steel.

This old photograph from Fred's album shows a mill chimney falling to earth.
Events like this inspired the young steeplejack.

Fred Dibnah

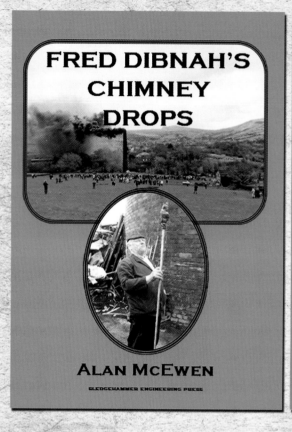

Author Alan McEwen, a retired Master Boilermaker and Steam Engineer well-known in the industrial heritage and steam world was a close friend of the late Master Steeplejack and Chimney Demolition Expert Fred Dibnah M.B.E. for close to 25 years, and within this beautifully produced book he has passionately and vividly chronicled 28 out of Fred's 90 amazing and often spine-tingling, dangerous chimney toppling exploits. Alan accompanied Fred on numerous extremely exciting and dangerous chimney demolition jobs all over North Western England, which enabled him to write the only authoritive account of Fred Dibnah's chimney toppling exploits.

This highly acclaimed book has received several brilliant reviews. This brilliant book chronicles 28 of Fred's amazing and often exceedingly dangerous chimney drops. Over 250 black and white and colour illustrations.

Great Value at only **£24.95** + £2.05 (U.K. Only)
Post and packing. Each Book
(please allow 14 (up to) days for delivery

IMMEDIATE DESPATCH

BOTH BOOKS A4 SIZE HARD BACK QUALITY PUBLICATIONS
200 PAGES, WRITTEN BY WELL-KNOWN BOILERMAKER
ALAN McEWEN AND PUBLISHED BY
SLEDGEHAMMER ENGINEERING PRESS LIMITED
PUBLISHERS OF QUALITY BOOKS ON BRITISH INDUSTRIAL HISTORY

HISTORIC STEAM BOILER EXPLOSIONS

HISTORIC STEAM
BOILER
EXPLOSIONS

ALAN McEWEN

SLEDGEHAMMER ENGINEERING PRESS LTD

HISTORIC STEAM BOILER EXPLOSIONS includes basic histories of early industrial boilers such as: Balloon or Haystack, Waggon, Rastrick Vertical, Egg-Ended, Cornish, Lancashire, Scotch Marine Return-Tube; unfired pressure vessels called Kiers, as well as Locomotive Boilers and Marine Rectangular or Box Boilers.
The writing of this book - HISTORIC STEAM BOILER EXPLOSIONS - the first modern publication for decades that authoritively chronicles early British industrial boiler explosions, has been a long time coming for author, Alan McEwen, a qualified Boiler Engineer, now retired, for he has spent well over 30 years researching and gathering material, including many rare photographs, that has made the publication of this book a reality.

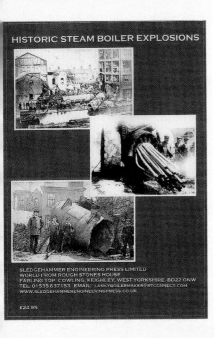

Within his book, Alan has chronicled 23 highly dramatic and informative stories based on his extensive research of the terrifying and devastating boiler explosions, including multiple explosions, that claimed the lives of hundreds of people whilst destroying the neighbouring buildings in Cotton Mills, Bleachworks, Collieries, Ironworks and other industries of the 19th and early 20th centuries. Included also, are 11 accounts of Traction Engine, Railway Locomotive and Marine Boiler explosions.

HISTORIC STEAM BOILER EXPLOSIONS is effectively two books in one.
Over 170 black and white illustrations.
£24.95 + Post and packing UK only £2.05 per book.
(please allow 14 (up to) days for delivery

We accept payment by most credit/debit cards, cheques, cash and postal orders made out to
SLEDGEHAMMER ENGINEERING PRESS LTD

WORLD FROM ROUGH STONES HOUSE, FARLING TOP
COWLING, KEIGHLEY,
WEST YORKSHIRE,
BD22 0NW
UNITED KINGDOM

Email: lankyboilermaker@btconnect.com
Web Site: www.sledgehammerengineeringpress.co.uk
Tel: 01535 637153

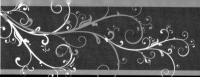

At the top of Bury Parish Church. Fred said that when you're high up and you have a good wind blowing around you, a cigarette lasts half as long as it would if you were on the ground.

Looking down on Lancashire graveyards I would say most are in poor condition with long grass and willow herb growing all over them. There is little or no attention paid to them. So I like the idea where the best tombstones are put up around the outer perimeter and the rest of the place covered in good green turf.

Other odd jobs I have to do from time to time include cleaning pigeon droppings from the tops of church belfries and mending clocks stuck way up on the tops of towers. Often I have to do both jobs at the same time and also put up wire netting up to prevent the pigeons returning to that particular toilet.

Now a funny thing happened on one of these jobs and it were a bit of a coincidence as well. Me father often used to help me after he had retired and we were high up in a church tower fixing some wire netting. Well it was about 11.30 one morning and we were banging away when I heard shuffling up the spiral stone staircase to the tower. The vicar then appeared and said, "Would

The vicar then appeared and said, "Would you stop hammering at about 11.45 as I have a funeral then." Of course we agreed and I asked whose funeral it was.

you stop hammering at about 11.45 as I have a funeral then." Of course we agreed and I asked whose funeral it was. When we were told, my father quickly sat down all thoughtful. You see it were the man he had worked for, for over 40 years. So we watched with special interest when the cortege arrived for the big man's funeral with a lot of black limousines and the men in tall hats. Me dad remained thoughtful but I took no more notice because funerals had become everyday occasions to me.

As I could not continue putting up the wire netting, I turned my attention to the church clock, which I also had to mend. It had been beautifully made by a man called Bailey in Manchester and run well for many years, until something went wrong with the chiming mechanism. I soon saw what was wrong with it. The weight, which drove the mechanism, had come off its pulley wheel and was resting on the spindle. So I said to my dad to rouse him from his morbid thoughts, "If we can get that baulk of wood out of the corner, it could go across the top of the box to help lever up that weight." Here I should explain that all the weights were suspended down an 80ft long wooden shaft, from where we were to the bottom of the tower. The weight in question that were giving the trouble, was about level with the top of this shaft, so it could be levered like I suggested.

We got the baulk of timber and put one end under the weight. My plan of campaign was to balance the timber across the top of the shaft ledge. Then when me dad held the weight upwards I would simply slip the wire from the spindle back on to its proper pulley. Meanwhile they were just getting the coffin out of the hearse in front of the church. "It's no good," said my father after straining away. "The ledge of the shaft is not high enough for the necessary leverage." "Yes," I agreed. "It needs another 3 or 4in like that half brick there."

So I picked up the brick, put it on top of the ledge and me dad again set about levering up the weight. This time he did it and I was able to replace the wire on its pulley. But we forgot about the half brick. As the baulk of wood was being removed, the brick fell off the ledge and went straight down the 80ft wooden shaft. By this time the coffin was entering the church and things were becoming solemn among the congregation. No one but the vicar knew we were around and everyone else were concentrating on other matters. Well you can imagine that 80ft of wooden shafting makes quite a good sounding box, and amplifies everything no end. There was this almighty crash which stopped the coffin bearers (halfway up the aisle) moving in their tracks, the organist stopped in mid note and everyone were looking around ashen faced. I looked down and could see them all sort of frozen like statues, I were a bit shaken like myself. Not so me dad. A slow smile spread over his face, which were stuck close to mine. "What are you thinking?" I whispered and, he whispered back, "They must think he's woken up," he said.

Apart from a passing interest in funerals, weddings and similar services, steeplejacks waiting in churches have other priorities. The main one as I have mentioned is the weather. It can be very frustrating whenever there is rain and it does that a lot around Lancashire. If, for example, you are pointing some coping stones up a steeple, what people call a nice drop of afternoon rain can ruin your whole morning's work.

A steeplejack 200ft up in the air also sees the weather from a long way off. He can watch it over the next town arriving there, giving them a downpour then leaving

their roof tops all bright and shining in the sunshine while it comes your way. There is a sort of inevitability about it which requires plenty of patience. I remember on one occasion how I spent many hours pointing some 30ft of coping stones at an incredibly difficult part of a church tower. Then the rain came and within seconds washed out every bit of mortar. You would never think I had ever done the job. So what happens next is that I have to do the same job all over again. That means going down to the graveyard tap where ordinary people get water for flowers and steeplejacks more water for more cement. On this occasion I did the job again and then it rained again. In the end I did that job three times in one day.

Another photograph of work in progress as Fred repairs the top of an unstable chimney.

In physical terms it means going up and down ladders with the thin handles of heavy buckets digging into your muscles. Recently after one of my television appearances I received a letter saying how lucky I was to live such a tranquil life high above all the cares and troubles of this world. I was very tempted to reply "You must be joking" but there was a grain of truth in the letter. Yes I like my job and I do have close ups of the wonderful work built by my ancestors. It is an incredible one if you think about it.

Within a very short span of time, they put up those six-storey mill houses, 250ft chimneys, huge churches and town halls, laid railway lines, dug canals and mined coal, not to forget building those endless rows of terrace houses with pubs and corner shops.

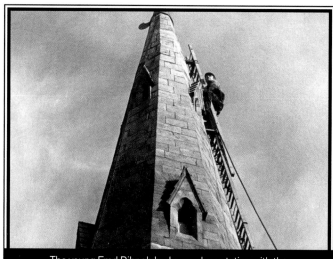

The young Fred Dibnah had a good reputation with the clergy of Bolton and soon found that he was working on many of the churches in the area.

This photograph held a special place in Fred Dibnah's heart. The photo was taken on the first day that Fred secured himself to one of the four gables on Bolton Parish Church in November 1963.

In those days the bosses had good suits, wore hats and carried gold watches. Next you look at the men with their sunken eyes in white faces.

You just cannot help noticing them when you are all alone above this incredible world stretching to the circular horizon. Just as you cannot help admiring the work that went into a single chimney stack, or a church steeple. I have seen them from close-up and they are fantastic. Great big stones perched 200ft up in the sky covered in incredible carvings. And all fitting perfectly in an attempt to try to keep them up there forever.

That is why I try hard to preserve things. I do not get much pleasure from demolishing a chimney because I always think of those fellows manhandling tens of thousands of bricks and tons of mortar to build the thing in the first place. It is the same with the churches and other buildings. They were not built by one or two keen religious types but must have required a swarms of your ordinary working men.

Then you come to the other side of the coin. You can catch a glimpse of it in those old sepia photographs of the bosses and their work forces from another age. In those days the bosses had good suits, wore hats and carried gold watches. Next you look at the men with their sunken eyes in white faces, in thin vests and ill-fitting trousers over their skinny frames. They were literally worked to death in those mills and factories, also hacking out seams of coal for 10, 12 or 14 hours a day in spaces less than 2ft high.

Fred's scaffolding at the top of Bolton Parish Church in November 1963. His work included pointing and long overdue attention to the weather vane.

So those Victorian bosses, all living in beautiful mansions would erect churches to salve their consciences. They were not all bad, but they all benefitted from other peoples misery. No-one got proper wages, there were no unions, no pensions and that was their creed. You just did as you were told and, like I said, worked yourself to death. Fortunately a few, like me dad, got through his 40 years of the filth in the bleach works despite the rats having a go at his dinner every working day.

There was another old friend of mine who came from a family of steeplejacks and had been one himself for decades. I remember him when I was a little lad, coughing and choking from the work he did on factory chimneys. There were no safety conditions then or a Welfare State either, but he managed to survive and put a bit by for his old age. "I got through it, Fred," he once told me, "and now I am going to enjoy taking things easy." The next day he was knocked over and killed by a lettuce wagon going to market. You cannot help having odd thoughts doing the odd jobs we steeplejacks do.

"I got through it, Fred," he once told me, "and now I am going to enjoy taking things easy." The next day he was knocked over and killed by a lettuce wagon. going to market.

BRICKS, ASHES
SAND, SOIL

TELEPHONE · WESTHOUGHTON 3147

GROUND MORTAR
RED SHALE (GRADED)

M.C.WALKER

& SONS (WESTHOUGHTON) LTD.
CONTRACTORS

FOR HIRE OR CONTRACT, HAULAGE TIPPING LORRIES.
PLANT HIRE & DEMOLITIONS.

PUBLIC WEIGHBRIDGE
CHURCH STREET DEPOT, WESTHOUGHTON
DIRECTORS: M.C.WALKER, L.WALKER, M.HEYWOOD

DEMOLITION

WIGAN ROAD
WESTHOUGHTON

Mr.F. Dibnah,
Steeplejack
8, Alfred St.,
Burnden Park,
Bolton.

14th Jan.1963.

Dear Sir,

We have pleasure in confirming the following plant hire rates:

Hire of loading shovels 1½ to 2½ cu.yd. -   35/- to 70/-
per hr.

Hire of lorries (4-wheel drive, and up
to 10 tons capacity)   - 17/9d. per hr.

With further reference to the making good required at the
Top Storey Club, Crown Street, Bolton, and at various other sites, we
should be glad if you would arrange to meet Mr. Walker jnr. at 2.45 p.m.
tomorrow Tuesday 15th Jan. at the Top Storey Club. If this is inconvenient
for you, perhaps you would contact the writer with a view to making
another appointment.

Yours faithfully,
FOR AND ON BEHALF OF

M. C. WALKER & SONS
(WESTHOUGHTON) LTD.

DIRECTOR

A rare invoice to Fred Dibnah dated 14th January 1963 from M.C. Walker (Contractors) for plant hire rates.
Notice that currency is in the old Pound, Shillings and Pence.

...odern world stinks.

"I set out as a steeplejack in m[...]
to preserve chimneys. I've fin[...]
knocking most of them down."

Fred Dibnah
Chimney Pieces

As Fred was learning his trade as a steeplejack he would often attach a chute to the side of large chimney stacks so that he could get bricks and mortar to the ground safely.

It was my friend Ken the Halle violinist who introduced me to his Uncle John. Ken was an enthusiastic amateur so far as chimneys were concerned, but he could not give them his full attention on account of the Brahms and Beethoven stuff. John on the other hand was very versatile. He seemed to have done everything in life including playing rugby, mining coal and sawing stone blocks. Just the chap, I decided, to be my assistant.

Our first job together entailed demolishing a chimney for a firm at Croston, which is a little village on the way to Southport. Funnily enough, the factory made chimney pots. That was interesting while the awkward bit concerned the chimney we had to fell. It were in a tight position between the works and a river. The local water authority had only just cleaned out that river and they told me, in no uncertain terms, not to drop a single brick in it.

Work commenced and we cut away some of the base, we put in the wooden props and laid a fire round them. Then we went round and weakened the other side of the base. Tension mounted in Croston when we lit the fire and the props were burned away. However, the chimney went over just right and everything after that were a bit of an anti-climax.

Next came a monstrous chimney at a big spinning and weaving company. It was 200ft high, octagonal in shape with a square base and had beautiful moulding round everything. It was also 6ft thick. Hammering holes through 6ft of perfectly laid Victorian brickwork can be painful. John and I had to stick at it because once you have accepted a job it is yours until the end. The job after that was unbelievable – another 200 footer which had to fall along a 60ft wide slot. There was no way of avoiding it. A street lay on one side and a mill wall on the other. The owners and their insurers were not the only ones shaking in their shoes, I can tell you. John and I again did all the hand cutting work but very, very carefully this time.

The job after that was unbelievable - another 200 footer which had to fall along a 60ft wide slot. There was no way of avoiding it.

Demolition of a concrete chimney at a waste disposal depot. The chimney was showing flaws in its design after only two years in service. Fred classically said "Even the simple people knew something was wrong with the chimney."

I heard the newsman saying, "Here's a chimney that went wrong." I raced into the front room just in time to see a chimney come crashing down on a factory building.

The mill chimney was due to come down on a Sunday morning when there would be less traffic to divert. So that Saturday night, we checked everything before leaving work. The cuts had been made, the props were in position and the fire laid. That stack was ready and waiting to come down inside, I hoped, the slot was right, as my reputation was riding on the drop going exactly to plan.

The television was on when I arrived home and, while talking to Alison in the kitchen, I heard the newsman saying, "Here's a chimney that went wrong." I raced into the front room just in time to see a chimney come crashing down on a factory building. When the newsman said the place was in Yorkshire, my relief was terrific. It was not however a relief for the Yorkshire firm, who had got it so wrong. After being cut in two, that factory was shut and there were people out of work. That kind of thing upsets me. So you see we chimney fellers have our responsibilities to make sure we do our job right.

Sunday morning came with the police and the usual sightseers gathered around waiting for Fred Dibnah to succeed or fail. I took a last look at the yard, down which the stack must fall, with the side of the factory beside it. "Lancashire has got to do better than Yorkshire," I remarked to John as the fire was being lit. The flames rose, the props burned away and the stack fell in a dead straight line along the yard. A couple of factory windows were broken by bouncing bricks but they let me off with that. Nothing succeeds like success and pride comes before a fall, so they say. Not long afterwards, a council gave me an official order to dismantle a couple of chimneys. The first was within 19ft of a main railway line, so the council's order stipulated that this stack must be taken down brick by brick. Well, after my precision job at the mill, I had become a bit swell-headed. I went to see the first of the two chimneys and noted it leaned away from the railway. "We can do this one the easy way," I said to John and he agreed. After all, the other way would mean hammers and chisels for weeks. I chose a bank holiday Saturday to have a go at that chimney. There were not a lot of people about when we cut the fire hole, put in the props and set fire to them. The props burned away, the fire went out but still the wretched chimney stood there beside the railway line. By then darkness was on us and we had to leave it for the night.

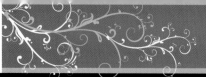

This was a job that called upon all of Fred's skills as a demolition man. He had to demolish the chimney straight down the side of a 7ft wall with only 9ft between the wall and the chimney.

You cannot help but be impressed as these photographs demonstrate that Fred got it spot on, and the chimney fell exactly where he had planned.

That night I rang Ken the violinist, his father and one or two other fellows about making an early morning start. We were all on site at 6am and by 8.30 the chimney was on the ground without a brick anywhere near the railway. It seemed that once again I had pulled off a perfect job. But someone must have seen and reported us for I received a very sharp letter from the council concerned. 'Dear Mr Dibnah,' it began unpromisingly, 'You have violated your contract, and also put us in a most critical position with the railway...' After reading that came chapter and verse ending with 'since you have broken your contract, it is now null and void'. Between this bad beginning and the even worse end, they mentioned I could not expect to be paid for the first chimney or even allowed near the second, despite it being situated in open country.

Ken Devine playing the violin in his local pub.

Fred with his 1927 AJS Motorbike. As his confidence grew he would ride the bike to factories and mills to drum up business.

Yet he was in the right. I had been contracted to take the chimney beside the railway down brick by brick. Instead I had felled it with an attempt at secrecy.

Now I knew one or two influential people and sought their advice on the matter. What each separately told me amounted to the same thing, "Creep," said one, "like mad, said another." "Write a letter in your best copper plate handwriting," the other said, "to the Borough Engineer asking for an interview."

Following my grovelling letter I was offered a formal interview. The chap who doled out demolition work for the council was there, and determined to shoot me down in flames. Yet he was in the right. I had been contracted to take the chimney beside the railway down brick by brick. Instead I had felled it with an attempt at secrecy. Therefore I had broken the contract as they said. End of argument.

More often than not, however, the best form of defence is to go off at an angle. I pointed out that many of the other chimneys felled in town by the explosive boys had gone wrong. My method, I pressed on, might seem old fashioned but the success rate proved its worth. "I tell you what," I said, 'I'll bring down your second chimney free of charge if you will pay me for the first one which is, after all, safely down." "Well..." the Borough Engineer nibbled at this bait, so I continued. "And you can light the fire yourself." He fancied the idea and we agreed on a certain Thursday.

On the day there was a Force 10 gale blowing. Normally I would have put the firing off and left the chimney 'on the sticks' as we say, but the big man from the town hall was still coming with all his entourage. Moreover the local newspaper happened to have been alerted and would be present to record the event.

So the Borough Engineer duly lit the fire and the newspaper photographers took pictures of him doing it. After that, no-one seemed to realise what was going wrong, except John and me. Besides burning the props, that high wind set fire to nearby grass and bushes. This caused the men from the council together with the press men to retreat some 200 yards. It left John and I gazing unbelievably up at the chimney. The props had long gone from the one side and the other had been weakened to ensure a fall, yet the stack stayed where it was. Or rather it swayed some 3ft this way and then 3ft the other way, like a willow wand.

It was crazy, it was dangerous and we had to do something. Hauling our 50 ton hydraulic jack out of the truck, we applied pressure. Fortunately we succeeded and the chimney came down to a ragged cheer from the distant spectators. When I went to talk to them, I told them that it were all about fine balancing and counteracting the high wind forces. As I said afterwards to John, "I had to make it look like we knew what we were doing." This brought me another job beside a railway line, which I would have preferred to have avoided.

Railway people are very alert and always suspicious of anything going on anywhere near their bit of track. In this case it were only a shunting yard and I thought we would have no trouble. But once more it was one of my minor disasters. There was not much about to harm anyone and one of my fellows had acquired some extra chimney fuel in the form of big rubber buffers. We packed these among the timber and then lit the touch-paper. Within minutes we covered the whole shunting yard in thick dense black smoke. Not only that, there was not enough heat being generated to bring down the chimney. We had to put out the fire and start again. It sounded simple enough until I discovered there was no water anywhere near the site. I searched frantically

Fred Dibnah posing for one of the hundreds of publicity photographs as his fame began to grow.

around and what I did find was a fleet of bulldozers each of which could take 45 gallons of water at a time. This they did, then tipped it over the flames beneath the chimney. The job had turned into a total shambles.

As soon as the flames were out, my men chiselled away six more inches of brickwork, we lit another fire and this time (without the rubber buffers) the thing came crashing down. Funny thing was it very nearly landed on a posh limousine which was coming our way at a critical time. Suddenly out stepped an equally posh character who said in a pained voice, "Do you people realise that you are interfering with the running of my railway." This put some of my fellows backs up and one said, "It ain't your bloody railway. It's supposed to belong to the nation." "Oh well," said the character before getting back into his limousine, "you've done a good job, but don't interfere with my railway again." I won't repeat what was said as he drove away.

After that, the chimney jobs I got to tackle seemed to be getting progressively harder. It may not seem possible, after all a chimney is a chimney, but there can be complications. The next job called for John and I to re-point a 200ft stack from top to bottom. This was a task which required erecting a lot of scaffolding then getting down to solid uninterrupted work. At the time, John was having personal problems and he had to leave me. He did so after most of the re-pointing was done, but it left me with scaffolding still up the chimney and no assistant to get it down. So who better to call in than my wife Alison. She left her house work and spent the next few days moving tackle with me. "You'll have to find another permanent assistant," she said at one stage and I said, "Yes, there is someone I have in mind," I told her.

That someone was Donald, who I have already mentioned in connection with the dangerous well which nearly killed me. His grandparents and parents once owned a big building company on the outskirts of town, but what happened to the family business was most unfortunate. The powers that be were building a motorway and compulsory purchased the entire premises. Donald was left with a house to live in and a bob or two at the bank but no business. He used to walk his dog past my place and we would get into conversation. "If you ever need a hand..." he had once said, so the time had come to take him up on it.

Our first job together was another council one. I should not say this, for all work is bread and butter, but town hall people can make a hard life harder for working men like me. And, when you get two lots of town hall people in on an act, it can become very tricky indeed when they get their heads together. In the end, you can spend more time and trouble than the job is worth.

And, when you get two lots of town hall people in on an act, it can become very tricky indeed when they get their heads together.

One of the remarkable ornate chimney structures that the Victorians left behind. Fred Dibnah enjoyed the challenge of climbing such chimneys so that he could see their craftsmanship up close.

In this particular case, two councils had gone about building a rubbish incinerator plant with a 200ft chimney. I do not mean using an old chimney, of which there were plenty about, but making a new one with all the resources of 20th century technology. Well that incineration plant was commissioned with a fanfare of trumpets. It was meant to be the greatest thing since sliced bread. True there were some teething troubles, but we can forget about that. Rubbish was being burned in the new technology chimney and within 18 months the chimney stack was cracked all the way up on both sides. That's when the in-fighting began. The project had been started by one council then transferred to the other. So, when it went wrong, it was somebody else's responsibility. Many of these councillors went to a pub I knew and one day as they were skirting round the subject, I asked when they were going to do something about that useless chimney.

They hummed and hawed about whether it was useless but, before long the stack had reached two years old, smoke was now coming out of it about 60ft from the top and even simple folk were saying, "What have they done now, like?"

Anyway, one day my phone rang. The call came from an engineer in the rubbish incineration plant. Could I come and have a look at the chimney? I went round and we talked about it for some time. In the end I said my ladders would have to go up in order for me to take a closer look at the crack and see how bad it was.

So I laddered their chimney and on a Sunday morning, when the fire was out, went up to carry out my inspection. The crack in the concrete was so bad you could put a packet of cigarettes in it, sideways. To prove it, I carried a camera with me and ran off three rolls of film. When these pictures were developed, everyone got all excited about them and agreed that the nearly new chimney would have to come down.

Fred's father Frank used to help Fred with some of his early jobs.

They hummed and hawed about whether it was useless but, before long the stack had reached two years old, smoke was now coming out of it about 60ft from the top.

One of Fred Dibnah's early steeplejack photographs as he worked between two buildings.

Fred and a friend high up at the top of a chimney stack. Notice the rows of terraced houses and the mill chimney in the background.

The bit about that job that I remember and which has always amused me, was some of consultants I had to consult. The council asked me to send my 108 prints to some real double barrelled architectural firm down in Middlesex, named 'Somebody, Somebody & Somebody'. "Dear Mr Dibnah', they wrote back, "please send us seven sets of all your photographs." To this day, I have no idea what they did with those 756 pictures, but you have to humour such people.

The trouble is you have to humour more and more people these days. It is no longer a simple matter doing what should be done. There are layers of people to get through: factory owners, property developers, council men and their consultants. The mill owners never have any money and the developers are always after quick money. The council people are experts in covering themselves, while the consultants seem to have it made. To make matters more complicated, most demolition jobs are put out to firms that specialise in them. I do the chimney side for a very good demolition company, but there are some real cowboys in that line of business. They tell you one thing and the authorities tell you another. Apart from risking your own life, dropping a chimney can do thousands of pounds worth of damage.

Apart from hitting buildings or falling across railway lines, there may be sewers or subterranean workings which would not take kindly to a 1,000 tons of bricks descending on them.

One cowboy outfit I remember had Donald and I start and stop three times on a job they had never wrapped up properly with the council. The head of the outfit, who wore a bobble hat, dark glasses and drove an Alpha Romeo car would keep telling me, "Not to worry Fred. I'll sort the bother out. Be on to you later this evening. Then a fortnight would go by before he rang again to say. "You can start tomorrow Fred." "As it happens I'm tied up tomorrow." "But this one is red hot urgent Fred. I've ironed out all the problems." When someone tells me that, I do begin to get worried. Once again we dropped everything and turned up on his site. Once more, nothing went according to plan. Again the king of the cowboys said he would sort out the council people.

So another week or two went by before he asked me to attend a site meeting. When Donald and I got there, it was to see two Irish lads hammering away at the bottom of the chimney. "Come on Donald," I said, "we've had enough of this." Fortunately we pulled out of that particular exercise.

The chimney finally fell over in the dark, ripping about 20 yards off a factory wall while the flying bits and pieces broke windows across the other side of the road. I am not trying to be clever or big-headed about all this. Few people realise the problems involved in chimney work, or the forces released when a stack comes down. There was one horror right in the middle of Bolton which illustrates my two points of problems and forces.

This chimney, that few people ever noticed or even thought about, was situated beside a mill and right next door to the market place. It had been built around 1860 to a height of 220ft. The brick thickness at the top was 9in and on top of that the builders placed a huge stone head. This capping weighed about 20 tons and had a 3ft overhang. They created what you might call a hundred-year time bomb. To be fair to the old builders, for the Victorians built well, their chimneys should have been regularly maintained.

"It'll do until next year," they would say, when their engineers dared to bring up the matter. So year after year, then decade after decade ticked by, with smoke gnawing away the insides of the chimney.

A crowd of hundreds gather for one of Fred's well advertised chimney demolitions.

It's hard to believe that it took only two men to construct a work area of scaffolding at the top of a chimney like this.

All the sulphurous and acidic smoke that goes up chimneys can be kept in hand by regular maintenance like inspections, new linings and general renovations. But Lancashire mill owners were notorious for not wanting to part with their cash. "It'll do until next year," they would say, when their engineers dared to bring up the matter. So year after year, then decade after decade ticked by, with smoke gnawing away the insides of the chimney.

There comes a time when you cant escape it – something has to be done. In the case of the particularly nasty chimney I had to put right, I would imagine the engineer had been told not to spend too much cash on it, which meant a patch job. So round the brick stack he wrapped what you might call an iron corset then he attached that to the factory wall by steel wires. I would lay a bet he was not even thanked for doing a cheap job.

Meanwhile the history of the country went on. There were business booms and depressions wars and outbreaks of peace. People were born, lived and died.

All the time, the chimney remained up there, unnoticed, taken for granted with the fumes passing through it and eating away more and more of the brickwork. Then one day, which unfortunately happened to me in my lifetime, a piece fell off into the mill yard as a kind of warning shot.

At long last, it was necessary to take positive action. "Fred's the chap," everyone said, "for this one." On reaching the top of the chimney and looking inside, I saw there was literally nothing left of the brickwork. I had suspected this when drilling holes for my ladder because the drill kept going straight through. The only thing which held up that 220ft stack, with its 20 ton capping on less than 9in of brick, were the iron corsets. By this stage people were saying, "We are leaving this entirely to you, Fred. It's your problem." I knew the way to do it, which is not the same as saying it was going to be simple. I would have to start my scaffolding some way down the stack then build a series of platforms with as many bracing pieces as possible, up to a stout support under the overhang. Then would come what you might call the moment of truth.

As a matter of morbid interest, three-quarters of the deaths among steeplejacks occur because of what can happen next. They would build their last staging support under the capping stones, then cut through angle ironwork to get at the stones themselves. At that stage the bloody lot would fall down smashing the staging and killing the men.

I managed to avoid this on that horror chimney by building substantial supports from strong pipes and stout pieces of timber. However, what nagged away at me all the time was the fact that the structure base on which my scaffolding and staging had been mounted were rotten. There was an ominous quiver when I cut the iron ring under the stone overhang, but as I lived to tell this tale you will have gathered that everything held. After that, Donald and I were able to get the chimney top capping stones down one by one, we then gently dismantled the rest of this horror stack. However, a funny thing happened during the otherwise precarious exercise. Whenever I am on particularly difficult jobs, there are always

Fred Dibnah at the top of a chimney stack, that has to be reduced in size by 30ft.

By this stage people were saying "We are leaving this entirely to you, Fred. It's your problem."

important looking people superintending and keeping an eye on progress. They generally drive big Mercedes cars and carry real leather brief cases with brass corners on them.

One such character always seemed to be around when Donald and I were putting up ladders. As I have said that were not easy in this case, due to the rotten brickwork, so we were very cautious hooking on each ladder in turn. At the end of it all, this character came up to me and said, "I have always been intrigued as to how ladders went up chimneys." "How did you think they went up then?" I asked. "Well," he said, "I imagined they were put end to end and connected, before being reared up the chimney." Donald, who was standing nearby, could not help laughing but I managed to keep a straight face. "It would be a bit difficult," I pointed out, "holding your foot on the bottom rung while trying to heave the other 199ft upwards." "I suppose it would be," said the chap, which made me wonder how he came to own a bloody Mercedes.

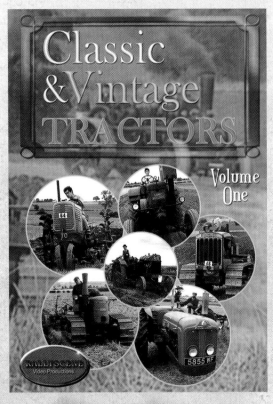

Fred's Steam Roller

Fred at a steam rally with his famous Aveling and Porter Steam Roller named Alison.

Fred, Alison and Betsy in front of the roller

Alison and the kids getting ready for a trip to a steam rally.

Fred with his own kind of roller.

Fred testing the Roller on Radcliffe road.

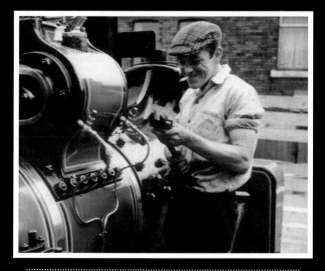

Fred working on his steam roller near his mother's house.

Fred outside his mother's house working on the derelict steam roller.

Fred smoking a fag, and reading some of the chapters in the original book ´Fred Dibnah Steeplejack´.

TRACTOR AND ROLLER COMBINED.
(Arranged for Rolling.)

Manufactured by AVELING & PORTER, LTD., ROCHESTER.

Original photograph from the Aveling & Porter catalogue showing the same type of steam roller that Fred Dibnah restored.

u make one
half a day
ndertaker."

BRIAR

"I've never fell off a big chimney...
You'd only fall off one of them o...

Fred Dibnah
Steam Engines

Fred working in his new engine shed at Radcliffe Road as he restores his steam roller to it's former glory.

Fred wins a trophy at a steam rally.

The television chap said my two passions are chimneys and steam engines. Chimneys, he said, could end my life and steam engines had come near to wrecking my marriage. It is true. I do spend more money on steam engines than the wife, kids and holidays. I have also neglected my business at times as well. Lots of people I have come across over the years say I spend too much time playing with my steam roller. You might have thought by now I had learned my lesson, but...

When I was very young, you see, I went every year to a fairground and there was this great steam engine that had wheels 7ft in diameter. It was lined up with the diesel engines and stood out like a pearl among swine. It fascinated me and I kept going back to look at its wonders. I went to that fair every year just to see the steam engine and one year it were gone just leaving the diesels. "Steam engine?" said a fairground man as if what I had seen never existed. "Oh, they're now obsolete, scrapped. Yon diesels are replacing them all." I found that very sad and it was the same when I visited the various mills and engineering works. At one time everything was run by steam. There were steam engines everywhere, little ones stuck in corners and big ones with their own engine houses for the hefty jobs, engines all huffing and puffing, turning belts and working shafts, so long as they had water and coal put in them.

Some truly magnificent steam engines were built towards the end of the 19th century and the beginning of the 20th for work in the mills. They were as I said put in their own special houses which were hard to enter. Sometimes even the mill owner and manager were banned from such places. You see, some of the engine men were crusty old types. They wore nice, well-washed engine driver's jackets and they ruled their domains as if they were emperors.

It fascinated me and I kept going back to look at its wonders. I went to that fair every year just to see the steam engine and one year it were gone, just leaving the diesels.

I could understand it. Everything depended on them to keep the mill working. They were in charge of engines developing 5-6000 horse power. These had up to ten boilers all in a row and the amounts of coal used were astronomical. That is why great tall chimneys were needed – it's also why Lancashire was covered in black soot. Steam engines were our industrial history and part of my inheritance.

At the time it seemed as if those wonderful steam engines would go on forever yet, one by one, they came to a stop. Now I only know of one left where it worked. It is connected to a big generator capable of supplying a factory with emergency light and power should the main electricity fail. In all other cases, when mills shut down, the steam engines are either left in their rooms never to run again or hauled to scrapyards for their metals.

Fortunately there are mill engine preservation societies that have managed to rescue engines, renovated and run them. But these are not the really big ones, only the quarter-sized things, which are just about transportable. To move one of those great steam engines would cost a fortune.

Polishing the roller before a steam rally.

A crowd of school children visit Fred's yard.

In Bolton there were three firms that made steam engines, lovingly and beautifully. They would put their nameplates on the engines because they were proud of their engineering abilities. When I were a lad admiring such engines, I never thought they would stop working and a nameplate would end up on my parlour wall. But then I never imagined I would also be demolishing the chimneys from above them. It is a strange world and I do not understand it.

People did not understand me when I bought a decrepit old steam engine and spent 14 years, and a bank full of money, doing it up. From the beginning, that engine of mine created all sorts of problems and heartaches. There was so much wrong with it I did not know where to begin. I would spend my days and nights trying to work out the problems, like how to cut, roll and drill one inch thick boiler plate, how to put rivets in that would hold.

Take the rivet problem, for example. As I asked about rivets, people became like that fairground man when the steam engine disappeared. I went round one engineering works after another enquiring, "Have you any riveters left?" "What? Who?" they would reply. Others told me, "All the riveters are dead." In the end I got the names and addresses of two men who had long retired. One of them had grown feeble but the other came and taught me the skill. I think he was pleased to hand it on. It were all he had left.

To give you some idea of the task I had set myself, it meant me having to drill 232 holes in the firebox alone with an ordinary ratchet drill. I would turn that handle hour by hour, with bottles of Guinness lined up beside me to help things along. Later I managed to pick up bits of equipment here and there that nobody wanted anymore, and now nobody else has. At first, however, I did everything the hard way. At least, as Alison used to say, it kept me out of the pub. She was right of course. Once I get my teeth into a job, I find it hard to let go. It were no use going to the pub, for this meant the job either became delayed or was not done that day. Sometimes I would think of going for just one pint, but I knew it would mean yarning with the lads. And if I did, all the while I would be thinking of those holes waiting to be drilled.

Working on steam engines is like serving a strange sort of apprenticeship. Because such engines were made in the Victorian age, so things have to be done in the Victorian way, which is the hard way like they did it. They were single-minded people when it came to getting a job done and it has made me the same. After my appearances on television I was often asked to give after-dinner speeches. Me, an after-dinner speaker! But it paid a little, which meant more money for my steam engine hobby. I cannot remember what I said to the Rotarians but that speech helped me to get two sacks of rivets.

I would turn that handle hour by hour, with bottles of Guinness lined up beside me to help things along.

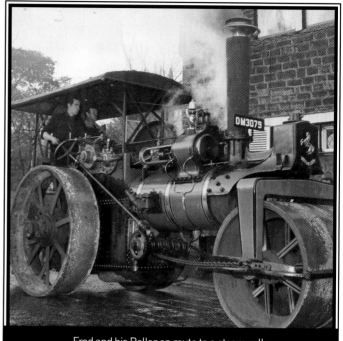

Fred and his Roller on route to a steam rally.

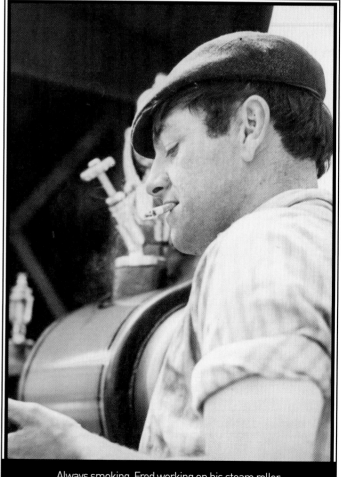

Always smoking, Fred working on his steam roller.

When I got my steam roller, I thought of calling it Thunderbolt for a joke. You see it could only do 4 miles an hour as it weighed all of 13 tons. Then I thought of naming the thing Alison. In hope to gain a bit of grace back by doing so. After all, there is not every woman who has a steam roller named after her.

Because of their speed, or lack of it, steam rollers take a long time getting anywhere. The funny part is we steam roller and tractor men find driving our monsters easier when we have had a few in us than when we are stone sober. Drink sort of eases the pain. For example, it feels less bumpy under the iron wheels and the racket going on becomes subdued. However, the main trouble with taking a lovely old steam roller for a run is that the roads are full of motor cars doing diabolical things. They do not seem to realise that though I can stop or start my roller, just like their motor cars, it must be done in a careful kind of way.

This can become a bit tricky when approaching traffic lights. Such lights seem to always attract car drivers when there is a steam roller ahead. They must be in front of the steam roller in order to get smartly away from the traffic lights. So they nip between the red light and my monster. What they do not seem to realise is that I am unable to see exactly where they are while I am trying to bring my steam roller to a stop. If they knew the peril they were in, such drivers would think twice.

Oiling the gears of his mean machine.

Fred's steam roller and living wagon. Notice the Greenall's brewery sponsorship on the side of the wagon.

Another source of trouble arises from the genuine interest people have in steam engines. As they whizz past me in their motor cars most drivers turn round. That means they are driving forwards but looking backwards. Once I was going up a long hill at the top of which a bus stood at a bus-stop. The driver of the car which overtook me was so interested in my steam roller, he drove right the way up that long hill, looking round at me all the time until he ran into the back of the bus.

Steam engines do not have to call at petrol stations, but they do need plenty of coal and water. The authorities do a Nelson, turning a blind eye on my activities, but really it is illegal to take water from hydrants. You can apply for a licence though, in my opinion, they should pay me a fee for testing their water hydrants because half are out of order. At least I put them right before carrying on with my journey.

My particular engine will do 7 to 8 miles on 80 gallons of water. So I have to use what I can get. It generally ends up with me calling the wife and kids to rally round and help with this urgent family matter. Lucky they do because if the level went too low there would be an explosion waking up the unlucky neighbourhood I happened to be passing through at the time. If you have a steam roller or traction engine, you will need a great caravan at the back, like a sort of support vehicle. Mine has beds under which I put the coal and cupboards for my oil cans. It also holds my wife Alison, the kids, our dog and a little corner cupboard for the jam butties. The dog quite likes my steam roller and he often sits on the board at the front, I presume to see where he is going. This means he can jump off at any time and, as we roll along he changes colour from white to dirty grey.

In the early years of our marriage, things looked a bit fraught between Alison and I where important matters like steam engines were concerned. To tell the truth, we were quite often close to divorce proceedings. Fortunately as our married life rolled on, my wife Alison

Alison the steam roller at Burtonwood steam rally.

became used to my other wife, Alison the steam roller, and even began to like her, I think. Mind you, men who fancy steam engines can be a bit peculiar, very few of the ones I know are married. They seem to think that wives and steam engines just do not mix. Worse still, they tend to look down on any woman, wife or not, who tries to get into their steam engine circle.

"Women," they say, "cannot begin to appreciate a steam engine." Worst still, they try getting their husbands to sell engines for mere money." Which I know has happened. But after that, a steam engine man is finished. His eyes go dull. Therefore I would never get rid of my steam roller. In fact, I have my eyes on a tractor which goes 16 miles an hour on rubber covered wheels. To me that represents a whole new dimension.

However, getting back to steam engine men, I would meet them at fairs and rallies, then naturally ask them back to my place for a drink and a chat. Also, on the way to my place or to theirs, we would have a few drinks to pass the travelling hours away. I remember one instance when two of us were drinking and driving at four mile per hour through the long night. The steam engine chap I had with me became so drunk he fell down on the back of the engine.

Early colour photograph of Fred Dibnah just after he became famous.

He were a huge fellow, over 6ft tall and wore size 15 boots which stuck out the end of the tarpaulin I put over him. I was still trundling along quite happily when all of a sudden the quiet road became a hive of activity. Police cars kept appearing and skidding to a stop until they surrounded me. It were lucky I could stop as well and none of them got squashed. Then about a dozen policemen came towards me, all serious like, with the sergeant in charge the most serious of all. I thought, 'Fred, this is definitely it.' So I thought of a plan before that very serious looking sergeant could have his say about my condition, the bottles rolling around the floor, not to speak of the unconscious figure.

I asked him about my steam roller, "Do you like these things?" You should have seen his eyes light up. He was like a little lad all over again, a boy with a new toy. I went on, "Would you like a go?" and his eyes went even bigger. At last he spoke, "Can I... can I drive it?" "You can't drive it," I said sternly, "but you may steer it. Under my supervision of course." "Of course, of course," he said humbly, then helped me to shift

We trundled up a long hill into town with the rest of the squad escorting us. By then it were dawn and the sun was rising.

the steam engine chap, who had begun snoring, out of our way.

By this time all the other policemen were smiling and relaxed. I suppose it makes a change from heavy crime to come across a minor Victorian felon like me. Well that sergeant steered for about four miles, which took an hour. We trundled up a long hill into town with the rest of the squad escorting us. By then it were dawn and the sun was rising. It shone on that sergeant's face and I have never seen anyone so happy. At last he turned to where I was sitting on the other side of my snoring friend and he said, "Thank you. Thank you very much." So I say to myself, steam engines cannot be that bad if they give people such pleasure. There have got to be worse things in life.

Fred and his steam roller hauling a flat wagon at Burtonwood steam rally.

A promotional photograph of Fred Dibnah and his steam roller outside Bolton Town Hall.

A steam engine also gives a kind of immortality, especially if you have resurrected one from a pile of rust. It does me good to know that after I am dead and gone, my steam roller will still be around. Even if some lunatic drops the bomb, it needs to be a powerful one to knock over Fred Dibnah's steam roller, I can tell you. Maybe the survivors will say, "Let us connect up to that wheel there to do a bit of belting," and they would be in business. They might build an engine house round my steam roller with a brick chimney above. As I have said, it is a strange world.

Every year I go to the great steam engine rally at Chelford, which is in the foreign fields of Cheshire. It is an epic journey with five hundred weight of coal under the beds, 80 gallons of water in the tank and a relentless pace of 4 miles an hour. Usually I get this great pile-up of cars behind me, though most seem to like steam rollers. Ever so often, however, there will

To me, driving through the countryside is rather boring because of all those fields. I was born and bred among streets, factories and chimneys.

be an impatient fellow hooting away somewhere along the line. That makes him a marked man as far as I am concerned. I know he is going to try overtaking the lot of us at the next straight stretch. I also know he will toot his little horn when accelerating past me. I therefore watch his approach and, just when his car is going past, I blow my steam whistle at 200 pounds per square inch. It is so loud it can be quite a shock to the nervous system, and usually makes them think about what they are doing.

To me, driving through the countryside is rather boring because of all those fields. I was born and bred among streets, factories and chimneys, all of which are interesting and different, while one field looks like another. It is the same with trees. I can tell the difference between say, oak and elm, but one elm tree looks very much like another elm tree, especially when you are rolling past at walking pace.

Then there is the noise aspect. Some engines with worn gearing make it impossible to speak to anyone more than a foot away, except in sign language. Others are really noisy and you can hear them coming for miles. Imagine if you are driving such a machine. You are in a noisy world of your own. .

Mine is not particularly bad but, after a few miles, it does leave me stone deaf. At least it has not done me any harm compared with the oil problems. The drops of oil being slung around get in your eyes, making them sore. On the other hand it is a good way to know the engine is running properly. If the oil being spread about turns from nice and warm to red hot, there could be trouble. Too much sunshine is another source of trouble where steam engines are concerned.

After a long run on a sunny day, everything becomes too hot to touch. Even the footplate turns into a sort of frying pan cooking your feet inside of their boots. That is why steam engine drivers always prefer to travel in the pouring rain. They are under a good sized roof and the rain on the rest of the engine acts as a sort of water cooling system.

Unfortunately rain can cause problem, particularly for steam rollers. Because there are no rubber tyres, the wheels and rollers will slip on wet, hilly roads or when you are trying to stop. Going down hill can be bad, especially if there are any metal manhole covers. Once a steam roller starts skidding it becomes a monster. That is why I have good brakes on mine to keep it under control.

I have only had two near disasters with my steam roller. The first was when I had a surplus of stones, which a very posh restaurant decided they wanted to buy, provided I could deliver them. So I said to them, "I'll deliver them by steam power." "You're joking," they said. "I am not joking," I said, so just to show them, I loaded a big trailer with all the stones. The load came to 20 tons and I set off for this restaurant place which was some miles outside Bolton on the moors. The road is very steep one-in-seven, which is like approaching Mount Everest for a steam roller. However, I made the outer journey all right apart from burning some of the paint on the funnel.

Once a steam roller starts skidding it becomes a monster. That is why I have good brakes on mine to keep it under control.

The new Dibnah headquarters on Radcliffe Road, Bolton.

It took some time to unload 20 tons and by then night was falling. So I lit the oil lamps and set out on the return journey. I thought getting back without the load would be simple. But, as I came travelling down that hill the crankshaft seemed to be going round a bit too fast. The next thing I knew was, instead of the wheels rolling properly, they were sliding like a sledge. I was tobogganing on a runaway steam roller from one side of the road to the other. By then the speed had increased to 25 mph which for a steam roller is fearful. I knew that halfway down the hill there were a corner and I also knew there was no way I could get round it. When I reached the corner, my runaway monster went straight across the road and into a field. A flat field might have helped but this particular field had even more of a slant than the road. At the far end of the field there was a 14ft drop into the back of a geriatric hospital. Fortunately, I

Instead of the wheels rolling properly, they were sliding like a sledge. I was tobogganing on a runaway steam roller from one side of the road to the other.

Fred in full steam on his way to a promotional event.

The Roller proudly showing off the name plate "Alison" after it was named after Fred's first wife.

hit a stone pillar which shattered, sending bits of rock high into the sky. My steam roller was also knackered. The front of the boiler dug 18in in the ground. If the roller had got away it would have smashed into the hospital like one of them bouncing bombs in the Dambusters.

My second near disaster, though it were not my fault, happened at the Chelford steam rally. Among the attractions, they had stuntmen who were always looking for more sensational tricks. One came up to me and said he was an escapologist. "I let people wrap 30ft of chain round me and then padlock the ends. Then I let them put me in a leather sack and padlock that. The trick I have in mind is when I'm in the sack and lying in the middle of the arena, I want you to try and run over me with your steam roller." "You must be mad," I said. 'No I'm not," he replied. "I can get out of the chains in seconds and escape from the leather sack anytime I want to. How long would it take your steam roller to reach the centre of the arena?" "Twelve seconds at the most, I said." 'No problem," he said. Well I thought about it and I was a bit apprehensive like, but the stuntman kept on at me. In the end we

A footplate view of the gears and workings of Fred's Steam Roller.

drew up a legal document saying that, if I squashed him flat, his widow would not sue me. He signed it at once and, after a couple more pints, so did I. But, as I sat on the steam roller watching the stuntman being chained, padlocked and put in the sack, I began to wonder what I had done. And would do.

They told me the announcer made a big thing of the event and the crowd became very quiet, though I did not know due to the engine noise. Later Alison said she shut her eyes. I could not see much either because after six

seconds the front of the vehicle blotted out my view of the wriggling man in the sack. He escaped by rolling to one side at the last second, still in the sack. I suppose stuntmen get their kicks, not so much because of the money, but from the danger and then the applause. I suppose I am a bit like that with my chimneys and steam engines.

That afternoon at the Chelford rally, I won a special prize for possessing the steam vehicle that had travelled the greatest distance under its own power. I often think of the friends that I have made through steam engines. I generally meet them outside their houses when I am grovelling in the road filling up with water. After that I tend to call on them year after year, and some have become friends for life. They insist on giving me cans of beer, which I cannot refuse, and they also seem to like me going into their posh houses to use their toilets.

That afternoon at the Chelford rally, I won a special prize for possessing the steam vehicle that had travelled the greatest distance under its own power.

"...m engines don't answer
...ou can belt them with a
...er and they say nowt."

> *"I have a wash more ne...*
> *I used to y'know... I h...*
> *shower everynight."*

Fred Dibnah
Funny Snippets

Smoke bellows out of this square brick chimney for the last time.

I am a Victorian. I don't do things like going shopping, you know. I went into a shop the other day and I had to walk out. I got that upset with the woman behind the counter.

Traction engines are good things because they don't answer you back. You can belt them with a hammer and they say nowt.

Having steam engines for a hobby makes a lot of work. Often I am in my workshop until one in the morning. After nine at night, I contain my hammering. At least I leave off the heavy blows out of respect for my neighbours. Donald who lives 200 yards aways says he can hear them in his parlour. So I have to think about my nearest neighbour who is only 20 yards away. Mind you, his house is up for sale.

There was a steeplejack called Mr. Smith and he lived in Rochdale from about 1860-1905. In those days the chimney, around Lancashire were like blades of grass, which made it the golden age of steeplejacking. This fellow Smith christened himself the Lancashire Steeplejack. He claimed to be the man who invented the method of scaling a factory chimney. It is quite possibly true. Before 1850, chimneys were about 90 feet high, then the Victorians began to build 200-300 footers. By the end of the century they needed mending and steeplejacks had a lot of trouble climbing them.

In Bolton we once had the biggest chimney in the whole of England. It was 34ft wide at the top, and 127ft in circumference at the base and an amazing 369ft tall. There was only one other taller chimney in the whole of the British Isles and that was the Townsend chimney at Glasgow, which was 490ft tall. I would loved to have climbed that one.

During the 1970s there were government sponsored people calling themselves church cleaners. They would arrive, encase the church in scaffolding, break a million slates on the roof and then shoot steam all over the place. These mindless people did more damage to our heritage in 10 years than a 100 years of industrial activity could ever have done.

In the town of Haywood they had England's answer to the leaning tower of Pisa. It were a 200ft factory chimney that was 5ft out of plumb. At one time this was the wonder of Lancashire. It stood there for years and its owners were rather proud of the freak thing. I don't know who knocked it down but it's gone now.

One fellow used to specialise in straightening curved chimneys. This was by no means an easy feat because, if anything went wrong, you could not run out of the way. He did this by cutting a series of horizontal slots then, with the help of iron wedges, putting thicker bricks on the convex side and narrower bricks on the other. He were a sort of inspired lunatic.

Thunder and lightning can scare you a bit when you're a steeplejack. On one occasion I was working up a 200ft chimney from which there was a rope all the way down to the ground. Rain had been falling all night and the rope was sopping wet. Suddenly I heard this kind of hiss and bang and saw the electricity travelling down that rope to the ground like along a high tension cable. Just seeing it were enough for me. I can tell you I went down the ladders almost as fast.

1930s chimney demolition.

Rare photograph following a demolition.

On another occasion I was up a church spire in a storm. Eventually I shot off the spire and got inside the tower, but that was still 100ft high. There was banging and crashing outside as if someone was trying to get at me crouching up there in the belfry. When the storm has passed over I went outside again and touched the lightning conductor. I nearly jumped back off the spire because the conductor was red hot.

It was half past eight on a Sunday morning at a place called Prescot near Liverpool. We had spent the Saturday preparing to demolish a dodgy 150ft chimney and I were surprised it had not fallen over during the night. As Donald and I were on our final preparations a policeman came up and asked, "Have you ever had any that went wrong?" People love disasters you know. "Well," said Donald, "on average one in every four go wrong, and we've just done three good ones."

Fred loads up with water on the way to a steam rally.

Now I think I can afford to buy a wreck and do it up like I did the last one. Those that are already done up and painted cost £15,000, which I can't afford.

Traction engines travel at about 16 miles an hour, which is four times faster than my steam roller. So I shall be able to get to rallies before my old age and not pop off on the way.

You have got to be a bit crackers to work on steam engines. It kills a lot of men off. Quite a few start with a great deal of enthusiasm. They are going to do this and that during the winter in preparation for next year's steam fairs. Which means working nights in their sheds like I do. After the first nasty winter, it is sort of bonk, and they have gone.

I am a compulsive cigarette smoker, you know. I have to celebrate with a cigarette and when everything goes right on a job, I am smoking all the time. Terrible things happen to cigarette smokers up chimneys. Like you have a packet of 20 in your top pocket,

bend a bit too much and you see them floating down to earth and usually straight into a puddle of water. That sort of stops me going down 200ft for another packet of ciggies.

Matches are another problem. When I am out of them I send a special signal to Donald who sticks three in the rope. Trouble is they tend to strike themselves on the side of the chimney on the way up. Then, having managed to light a cigarette, it is gone in a couple of minutes. You can see it glowing at the end because of the wind. Smoking is therefore a bit of a hazard but so is climbing chimneys.

All the old steeplejacks used to smoke. They would sit halfway up and have a puff, so I do the same. It is a wonderful sensation to put your back against the wall, halfway up to heaven as you might say. I think about what I am going to do with my steam engine at home and about the big problem awaiting me at the top of the chimney. I have solved a lot of them having a cigarette halfway up.

A relaxed looking Fred as he is filmed for his first documentary.

Fred using the roller wheel as a toilet.

There are also some unexpected hazards when working up church towers and steeples. More often than not a nesting bird will come zooming out of somewhere. I always treat them with the greatest respect because I know one of the damn things could kill me. It could happen in a split second. Next thing I could be rattling down the side of the church breaking off a few fancy bits on my way. After that I would have half a day out with the undertakers.

I believe in God. Sometimes I have a feeling he might know me like. "That's Fred Dibnah," he would say, "who keeps climbing up my church spires." Some days he does not like me. I drive 20 miles, climb 200ft and his heavens open. On the other hand, he has not let me fall off so far or let me drop anything to kill anybody.

My wife says, "You'll never fall off. There's definitely somebody watching you somewhere." She says I am better up aloft than on the floor. Quite often I trip over things on floors.

My sort of heaven would be a great place where nobody did any fighting or was hungry. In my part I would like a big pile of rusty steam engines and enough iron plate to mend them all. That would be quite wonderful because I would not have to worry where my next dinner was coming from. I could just get on with mending those ancient relics forever.

Some church vicars get in a bit of a huff with me. "You have had the job for weeks," they say. "When are you going to get on with it?" Unfortunately my job does not work their way. You see, they are speaking from the comfort and warmth of a vestry. They do not seem to realise it rains, blows and snows outside. So quite a lot send me letters starting, "Dear Mr Dibnah, if you feel you cannot get around to doing my job, I shall have to find someone else." I do not say much as their church spires have been falling to pieces or collecting pigeon shit for the last 20 years.

Fearless Fred Dibnah escaping the flames during one of his early chimney drops...

I rather like my oily flat cap. People ask me what is its flash point which isn't a joke really. When I am working with hot iron, it does go on fire at times and I have to whack out the flames.

If I go on holiday I find I must wear my cap or I feel as if somebody has shaved my head. Also, after days slogging over steam engines, I have actually been to bed in it. I also wear it going to the toilet. Well, Mark Phillips wears a cap doesn't he?

On one occasion I put rather a big dent on top of a brand new motor car. It should not have been parked in my brick disposal area round the bottom of a chimney. So in my opinion it was not my fault. I had picked up two bricks then the wind took off a nice big 6in piece of mortar. The piece went sailing away on the wind in a most beautiful arc before landing up on this fellow's new Volvo. He was not too happy.

I am sort of insured but if I kill any insurance officials looking up at me from down below, I am in dire trouble. It would be fair to say insurance men and me don't mix.

To them I am a bit like those racing drivers or that chap who jumps off cliffs on his motor bike. High risk they call it, which means jacking the premiums up. Still it makes them rich.

I'll never be a rich man climbing chimneys. There is no doubt about that. I would be better off owning a corner shop. On the other hand I am never broke because there is always somebody wanting me to do something silly. Like risking my neck.

I don't count money. I spend it as it comes. My wife can have what she wants and my steam engine called Alison is real greedy (always wanting money). Fortunately I think steam engines are better than money, like some people prefer old stamps or oil paintings.

This celebrity business is all very well if you could escape from it. For example, I never thought it took so many man-hours to make an advertisement for beer. We did 999 takes of me drinking beer in some club. I had to take a taxi home afterwards as my legs wouldn't work.

..and the only occasion that Fred wore a Top Hat during a chimney felling.

Official photograph marking Fred Dibnah's first television documentary.

Often I get fantastic phone calls such as would I hop over to Barbados and knock 50 feet off a couple of chimneys. Donald said he disliked camping so we did not go. Anyway me knees are knobbly and I would not look very good in shorts.

I built a chimney for me mum when I was 17 years old. We had a stack like the one next door. Four out of five pots were disused so I concentrated on making one good stack. I did not really design it, just built it. People said I was crazy but it never cracked and has a strong draught that would suck your slippers off.

My main competition when it comes to felling chimneys is from the dynamite men. They come along, 3-2-1, press a plunger, bang and that's it. Or there are the mad men. No pit props, nothing. They chop a hole out of the bottom, as if the chimney were a big old tree. They then keep bashing away until it is creaking and groaning, then they run out the road at great speed.

What they have done is they have just destroyed something which took a lot of men a long time, hard work, blood and sweat to construct. When those old builders finished the job, they were proud to place a Union Jack on the top. If you had, like I do, to take out three foot of brick when a few hundred tons is squeezing on it, then that chimney has not died so easy, has it?

I said I did not go much on insurance men. They send some lad out from the office, who has never seen a chimney before, to work out all the risks involved. I ask you. Yet they have got big new Mk10 Jaguars which they park next to my second hand army Land Rover. There is a moral in there somewhere.

Hundreds of chimneys reaching for the sky in this 1920s photograph.

Some funny jobs come my way because I have this reputation for working quietly and systematically. The local authority called me one day and asked if I would help them with a nature reserve. "We want you to lower an island without shattering the tranquillity of the place." You see, the nature reserve was being created in an old valley where there was wild fowl that have short legs and webbed feet. The fowl could not get on to the island on account of its sides being too steep. "Oh I see," I said when this was explained to me. "You want it levelling out a bit like Blackpool so they can just wander off the beach." "That's right," said the nature chap.

At one time the valley had been thick with coal mines, then it became a tip full of rubbish, rats and flies. When the wind was blowing, you needed a gas mask to go near the place. Now all is covered over by beautiful green grass and trees have been planted. In 20 years' time it will be as if men had never mucked it up in the first place. So there I was helping things along. I had to reduce the height of the island from its present 15ft tall to 3ft. It would have been easier to blow off the top by explosives but the fishes and wild fowl would not have

liked that. Therefore I did it silently, the old-fashioned way, with a shovel.

Sometimes when I am high up some chimney or church tower, I get illusions of grandeur. I look down on those humble rows of houses and say, "I am glad I'm up here and not down there inside one of your little places. Up here I am as free as a bird."

I often think my sort of life is more exciting than most people's. They never have anything exciting happen unless they go on strike.

Perhaps steeplejacking appeals to me because I am basically lazy. It is the sort of job where some days, when it rains, I am quite happy. You see it means I can stay home and work on my engines. Time passes pleasantly by that way. Now if I were working a machine in a factory I would watch the clock all the time. People often ask if I am not bored knocking them bricks off one at a time. Well, the answer is no. Because parts of my job are relatively simple, I carry on doing them while my mind wanders away to pleasant things, like I am at home mending steam engines.

The official Fred Dibnah stamp, which was hammered on to all of Fred's weathervanes.

I think I'll die when nobody wants me anymore. But I also think I'll carry on until I am an old fellow. I don't know but I suppose I'll slow down before I am 70. Instead of dying in bed I would like to drop off something on a nice sunny day and that would be that. Near my house is the cemetery where we all end up eventually. In there somewhere is the first and only man in Bolton to be killed by a lion, which is interesting. Also me dad used to tell me interesting stories about the place. How, when there was a great flood, one or two bodies were washed into the river. I don't know if there is any truth in it but I do know that in the river bed there are all sorts of gravestones. I would not mind building my own grave stone. It would be like a chimney with a staging round the top, lightning conductor and everything. Carved on it would be just the word Fred.

So much has changed since Dr Fred Dibnah M.B.E. wrote the book "Fred Dibnah Steeplejack". Written in a time when he was on the first steps on the ladder of fame. Little did he know that he would become one of the most famous people in the land.

It is wonderful to look back and remember the flat capped man from Bolton who became a national icon.

Dr Frederick Dibnah M.B.E. 1938 - 2004

Burtonwood Control Tower on its way down to earth.

...ng boys to bake cakes?
...no way to maintain an
industrial empire."

"As I sat on the steam roller
the stunt man being chained, p
and put in the sack, I began to
what I had done."

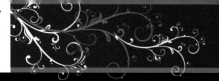

thing is nowadays, you'll
men working, yet 60 men
them *"You can't do that,*
u ain't got a tin hat on'".

AFC BOURNEMOUTH

THE OFFICIAL ANNUAL 2019

Written by Matt Joyce, Iain Pearce & Zoe Rundle
Designed by Chris Payne

A Grange Publication

ISBN: 978-1-912595-02-0

CONTENTS

AFC BOURNEMOUTH
2018/19

EDDIE & JASON
AGAINST THE ODDS

Long before Eddie Howe and Jason Tindall were plotting the Cherries' rise to the Premier League, they were top defenders for the club. What an adventure it's been in the last 25 years - let's have a look at the dream duo's route to the top!

Eddie was the first to introduce himself to the Cherries fans. He grew up in Verwood, was on the Dean Court terraces as a youngster and came through the youth system, first getting his chance in December 1995 against Hull City. He did a great job, winning the man of the match award and helping to keep a clean sheet as the Cherries won 2-0.

Two-and-a-half years later and Jason was also at Dean Court after arriving from Charlton. Coming into the defence he made an immediate impact, scoring a penalty on his debut as his new team beat Millwall 3-0.

Injury ended Eddie's playing career early, and by the time Jason hung up his boots the pair had over 550 Cherries showings between them... but their adventure with the club was just beginning!

In 2008 the Cherries were in a big relegation battle, struggling in the fourth tier without a manager and with a 17-point deduction to overcome.

Eddie was coaching in the youth setup and was called in to help as caretaker manager. Two games later he was given the job full-time, with Jason joining him as his assistant. The entire club's existence was at stake.

A huge haul of ten wins soon gave Bournemouth a chance at safety, and with two games to go the famous 2-1 win over Grimsby meant we'd done it – the Great Escape had been completed and Bournemouth were staying in the league!

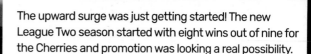

The upward surge was just getting started! The new League Two season started with eight wins out of nine for the Cherries and promotion was looking a real possibility.

Amazingly, even though Eddie and Jason weren't allowed to bring in any new players, Bournemouth sealed their return to League One with a memorable win away at Burton Albion, the Cherries were on the rise!

Soon Eddie had managed a century of games for the club, but his 100th match would be his last Bournemouth game for a while, as the management duo moved to Burnley to test themselves in the Championship.

2012

After 18 months with the Clarets, Eddie and Jason returned home to their former stomping ground – they were back with the Cherries!

The pair came back in October, and before 2012 was out they'd already managed more than ten wins – and they weren't done there, guiding the team to eight wins in a row in the spring to hop the Cherries up into the Championship for just the second time in the club's history.

Bournemouth did well in their first second-tier season, finishing in the top ten, but there was nothing to prepare the fans for Eddie and Jason's next trick – they had their eyes on the Premier League!

The 2014/15 season started well with a 4-0 win away to Huddersfield, and 11 more wins before Christmas meant that the manager, his assistant and all the Cherries fans opened their festive presents top of the Championship tree, but could they keep up the speedy pace?

Yes they could!

On a memorable night at Vitality Stadium Bolton were beaten and the Cherries knew they'd be in the Premier League for the first time the next season, and five days later they were champions! Eddie and Jason had taken the team to the top flight for the first time ever - an unbelievable achievement!

The management team brought in some new players as they had their first shot at the Premier League, but they also showed their faith in the players that had won promotion.

Against expectations, the Cherries stayed up in their first season, then they finished an amazing ninth, before finishing in mid-table last year in their third season.

Eddie and Jason are now taking on some of the world's best managers every week, from Jose Mourinho to Pep Guardiola, and proving that their side deserve to compete – and we've scored wins over Manchester United, Liverpool, Chelsea and Arsenal already in our Premier League adventure!

2018

LEAGUE OF NATIONS

ASMIR BEGOVIC

Born in: **Trebinje, Bosnia & Herzegovina**
Year joined: **2017**

Fun fact: Despite having a small population of approximately 33,178 people, it's one of the largest places in Bosnia and Herzegovina!

DIEGO RICO

Born in: **Burgos, Spain**
Year joined: **2018**

Fun fact: Burgos is a place full of history, being well known for its architecture and ten museums!

Colombia is a whopping **5,205 miles** from Bournemouth!

Heading into our fourth Premier League season, we're proud of the number of homegrown players we have in our squad, but we're also proud of the foreign talent we've recruited to join us on our top-flight adventure.

Here's a little look at some of the countries that are represented across the squad as we now have more players from outside of England than ever before.

JEFFERSON LERMA

Born in: **El Cerrito, Colombia**
Year joined: **2018**

Fun fact: El Cerrito translates literally into English as The Small Hill!

RYAN FRASER

Born in: **Aberdeen, Scotland**
Year joined: **2013**

Fun fact: The National Lottery has produced more than 40 millionaires in Aberdeen alone, making the city one of the UK's luckiest!

JOSHUA KING

Born in: **Oslo, Norway**
Year joined: **2015**

Fun Fact: Oslo is not only the biggest exporter of salmon, but it also hosts the Nobel Peace Prize every year!

NATHAN AKÉ

Born in: **The Hague, Netherlands**
Year joined: **2017 (permanently)**

Fun Fact: With a population of more than one million people, it is the third-largest city in the Netherlands, after Amsterdam and Rotterdam!

LYS MOUSSET

Born in: **Montivilliers, France**
Year joined: **2016**

Fun Fact: Montivilliers is close to Le Harve, but is a small farming town with a population of approximately 16,451!

ARTUR BORUC

Born in: **Siedlce, Poland**
Year joined: **2015 (permanently)**

Fun fact: Poland is the ninth largest country in Europe by land area!

COMEBACK KINGS

AFC BOURNEMOUTH 2
BRIGHTON 1

The home fixture with Brighton came at a crucial time for the Cherries, who were yet to record a win in their Premier League campaign. It was mid-September under the lights when Chris Hughton's side visited Vitality Stadium and Eddie Howe's men had lost their opening four fixtures.

It wasn't in the script when Solly March put the Seagulls into the lead with 55 minutes on the clock and the Cherries were a little over half-an-hour from a fifth consecutive defeat. Yet, with Jordon Ibe introduced, everything changed.

An assist almost immediately saw Andrew Surman finish well with 20 minutes to go, before a neat backheel for Jermain Defoe completed the comeback. It was an iconic moment for the striker, who was on loan with the Cherries in 2000, as the goal was his first since returning to the club.

An entertaining affair at Vitality Stadium occurred on Boxing Day, with six goals between the Cherries and West Ham. With nothing between the sides, it was all to play for between two sides occupying the lower half of the table.

James Collins ensured West Ham got off to a flying start, finding the net inside just seven minutes. However, Dan Gosling's effort before the break ensured it was all even going into the second half on a chilly afternoon at Vitality Stadium.

Following the interval, Nathan Ake rose highest and headed Bournemouth into the lead, before the Hammers were back on level terms through Marko Arnautovic with just ten minutes to go. It was the Austrian who then looked to have won it for the visitors, with an 89th minute goal to leave the score standing at 3-2.

Yet, a last-ditch effort from the Cherries was rewarded, with Callum Wilson at the back post to glide the ball past a diving Joe Hart. A point saved and a match to remember for the Cherries.

AFC BOURNEMOUTH 3
WEST HAM 3

12

AFC BOURNEMOUTH 2
ARSENAL 1

Stoke City sat in the relegation zone at the time of travelling south, with the Cherries keen to build on their January form, which saw wins over Premier League giants Arsenal and Chelsea.

Xherdan Shaqiri, however, put the visitors in front with just five minutes gone, as the Cherries had a game to chase almost from the off. Yet, the leveller didn't come until 70 minutes in, with Joshua King popping up from close range to find the target and ensure his side were back in the game.

And less than ten minutes later, it was young French striker Lys Mousset who found the net to give the Cherries the lead, heading home from close range for his first top flight Bournemouth goal. With just ten minutes to go, the hosts held on and continued their fine form of 2018.

AFC BOURNEMOUTH 2
WEST BROM 1

With the Baggies struggling at the foot of the Premier League table, they visited Vitality Stadium in March desperate for points. Alan Pardew's side arrived with just one win in their last 29 and relegation was looming, so when Jay Rodriguez's strike gave them the lead, the Cherries had work to do.

Consistent pressure from the home side eventually prevailed and the Cherries were back on level terms thanks to an excellent long-range strike from Jordon Ibe. With an international break to follow, both sides were keen to get three points under their belts before a two-week gap. And it took a moment of magic from Junior Stanislas to send the home fans into raptures.

With Joshua King fouled 25-yards out by Craig Dawson, Stanislas stepped up with a minute remaining. A sweetly struck free-kick flew into the top left-hand corner, with the winger wheeling away to celebrate with the Cherries bench. A moment to remember in the 2017/18 campaign.

AFC BOURNEMOUTH 2
STOKE CITY 1

One of the highlights of the season undoubtedly came against Arsenal. A fixture that the Cherries almost bagged three points from the year before, drawing 3-3 at Vitality Stadium. The Gunners, without star duo Alexis Sanchez and Mesut Ozil, took the lead through Hector Bellerin 52 minutes in.

But, Arsene Wenger's side were only ahead for 18 minutes, with Callum Wilson superbly poking home from Ryan Fraser's cross. With the scores tied at 1-1 and the Cherries pressing forward, it was Jordon Ibe who popped up for his first Cherries strike, thumping home from close range to give Eddie Howe's side the lead.

The win was the Cherries' first against Arsenal in the Premier League and was part of a memorable two weeks, which also saw the side win 3-0 against Chelsea at Stamford Bridge.

PAST, PRESENT & FUTURE

WITH NATHAN AKÉ

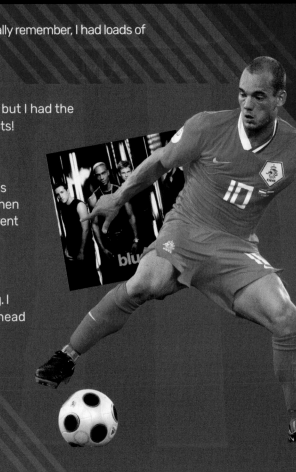

PAST

FIRST REPLICA KIT...

I never had a team as a kid, I just loved every team. I can't really remember, I had loads of countries and I just loved football – probably a Holland shirt!

FIRST PAIR OF BOOTS...

I think it was the Adidas f10 – they had f50s at the time but I had the f10s. They were black, we weren't allowed coloured boots!

FIRST FOOTBALLING HERO...

I didn't really have a footballing hero you know. When I was younger I used to watch people like Zlatan Ibrahimovic when he was in Holland, Wesley Sneijder, Andres Iniesta – different people not really one in particular!

FIRST RECORD BOUGHT...

I was like a music sponge, I would listen to a bit of everything. I don't remember really but the first band that came into my head were Blue – so we'll go with one of their songs!

FIRST CAR...

An Audi A3.

WHO IS YOUR BEST MATE AT THE CLUB AND WHAT IS THEIR ANNOYING HABIT?

I chill a lot with Lys and Jordon and before Brad Smith went out on loan I chilled a lot with him as well. Brad's annoying habit is when you sit in a room and play computer games, it is always properly serious, no fun!

BEST LUNCH AT THE TRAINING GROUND?

Simple, rice, chicken, potatoes things like this. The chefs are good and it's all very healthy.

WORST THING ABOUT TRAINING?

When you lose.

WHO'S THE BEST CONTACT IN YOUR PHONE BOOK?

Best or famous? I think the most famous would be John Terry.

WHAT MUSIC ARE YOU LISTENING TO AT THE MOMENT?

I like Drake, I'm still listening to his latest album Scorpion.

LAST FILM YOU WATCHED?

Mission Impossible, it's a cliché sort of film but it's a good film!

FUTURE

WILL YOU STAY IN THE GAME WHEN YOU RETIRE?

I'm not 100% sure, I'm not really a manager type I don't feel, I'm not sure.

WHERE WOULD YOU LIKE TO VISIT?

My dad's country, Ivory Coast.

WHAT SPORTING EVENT WOULD YOU MOST LIKE TO GO TO?

Wimbledon – I'm into tennis and it'd be great to go.

WHAT GROUND WOULD YOU LIKE TO PLAY AT?

Camp Nou – I've never played there.

WHAT HOBBY WOULD YOU LIKE TO GET MORE INTO WHEN YOU RETIRE?

Tennis, I play now and I would like to continue. I'm OK, not great but that can be improved.

DO YOU HAVE AN AMBITION THAT YOU WANT TO ACHIEVE IN THE FUTURE?

I've not even thought about it yet, it's too early for me now!

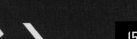

GAME CHANGERS

It's been a busy summer and the squad is bursting with quality and experience across all levels of the game.

Every one of our players has had a different pathway to where they are now in the 2018/19 season.

Some have enjoyed consistent top-flight experience at some massive clubs, while others have worked their way from the Football League to become Premier League players.

Along the way, many have had defining moments and games that helped change their career and put them on the right path.

Here, we look at five of our squad's standout matches in their stellar careers and you can judge for yourself what sort of an impact they have had!

So, Jordon Ibe, Ryan Fraser, Lewis Cook, Jermain Defoe and Callum Wilson... these are your Game Changers!

TOP 5

WITH JORDON IBE

Jordon Ibe's still in his early 20s, but his career's already taken him from his home in south London to breaking records with Wycombe, then moving to Liverpool, playing for England youth sides and finally switching to AFC Bournemouth.

We've already seen plenty of Jordon's best bits in red and black, but here we pick out five matches from across the winger's career so far.

IBE ARRIVES

Jordon may not have played a big part in this important League One win for Wycombe – he came off the bench in the 89th minute – but he broke a record just by coming onto the pitch!

The winger had already featured in three cup games for the Chairboys that season, and at just 15 years and 311 days he became the club's youngest ever Football League player against Hartlepool.

Jordon was clearly impressing his coaches, as two weeks later he made his first professional start and scored his first goal at home to Sheffield Wednesday – the football world was waking up to the young winger's talent!

Within two months of this Hartlepool match, Liverpool moved to bring Jordon to Anfield and, after working with the youth setup, the next season ended with a Premier League debut for the winger away at QPR on the final day of the season.

It capped off a rapid rise for Jordon in such a short space of time!

Hartlepool United 1
Wycombe Wanderers 3

October 15th 2011

ENGLAND'S HAT-TRICK HERO

Jordon has played for England throughout the age levels, and scored the first treble of his career for the under-19s in a big win against Montenegro.

The Cherries winger was in the squad with loads of other young stars who have gone on to play in the Premier League, such as Ruben Loftus-Cheek and Calum Chambers, and at Walsall's stadium the Three Lions lined up for what would be an easy win in a European Championship qualifier.

Jordon got the rout started in the West Midlands and then scored two more in seven minutes after the break to confirm the victory and further underline his potential.

As well as playing for the under-19s, Jordon later played three times for the under-20s and four times for the under-21s.

With some more good performances from Jordon to come, perhaps we'll see if he can push into the senior squad soon!

England 6   Montenegro 0 | May 24th 2014

ON THE EUROPEAN STAGE

Jurgen Klopp's reign as manager at Anfield was just underway and Liverpool's Europa League campaign was stalling in the group stage – until Jordon came up with the goods!

The Reds had drawn their first three games and faced a tricky 4000-mile trip to Russia and back to take on Rubin Kazan in November.

It may have been chilly, but Jordon warmed up the supporters with a man-of-the-match showing and scored his first Liverpool goal to win the match.

Aged 19, Jordon passed one man to receive the ball, sped past another and fired an unstoppable low drive in off the far post for the only goal of the game.

What did Klopp think of it? After the match he ran onto the pitch to give the evening's star man a big hug!

Rubin Kazan 0
Liverpool 1   November 5th 2015

ON LOAN & LEARNING

It's not easy jumping straight into the first team at a big club like Liverpool, so Jordon went out to get some experience in the Championship with the Rams.

Still a teenager when he arrived at Pride Park, Jordon fitted in well and was a menace to Championship defences with his speedy dribbling and attacking intent – scoring five goals during his stay with Derby.

This pace and power was in evidence at St Andrew's – with Birmingham City the other club Jordon enjoyed a loan spell with – when the young winger burst into the box, beat his marker and rifled home to get the Rams on their way to another big win that season.

In fact, when Jordon returned to Anfield in January, Derby were up in the heights of second in the table – behind only the Cherries in the standings!!

Birmingham City 0
Derby County 4
December 26th 2014

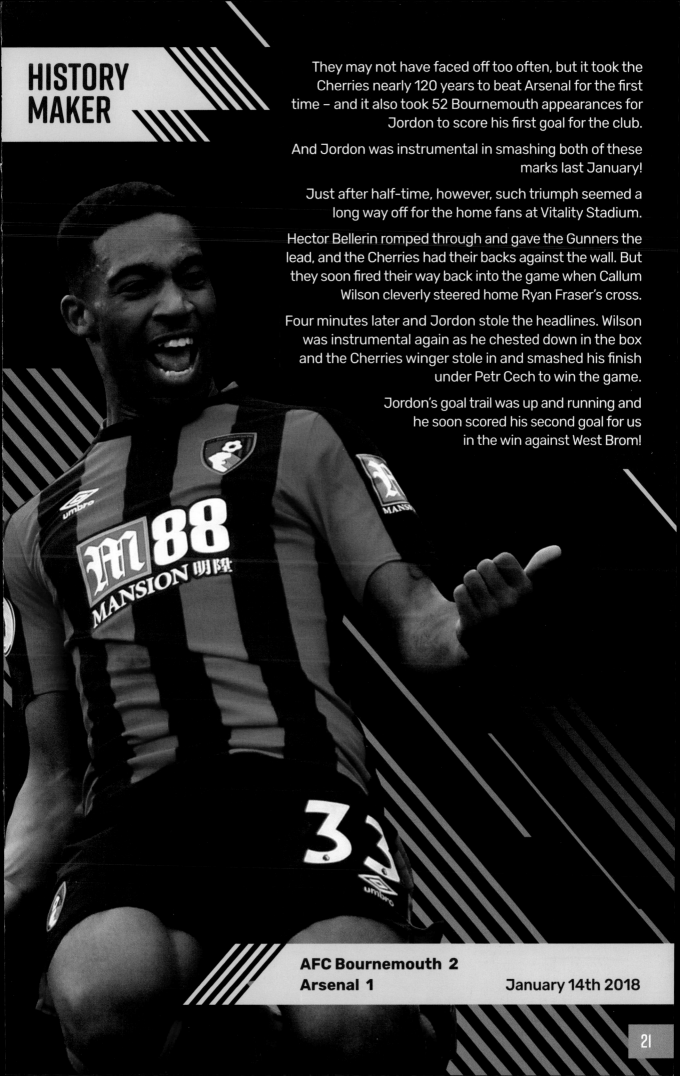

HISTORY MAKER

They may not have faced off too often, but it took the Cherries nearly 120 years to beat Arsenal for the first time – and it also took 52 Bournemouth appearances for Jordon to score his first goal for the club.

And Jordon was instrumental in smashing both of these marks last January!

Just after half-time, however, such triumph seemed a long way off for the home fans at Vitality Stadium.

Hector Bellerin romped through and gave the Gunners the lead, and the Cherries had their backs against the wall. But they soon fired their way back into the game when Callum Wilson cleverly steered home Ryan Fraser's cross.

Four minutes later and Jordon stole the headlines. Wilson was instrumental again as he chested down in the box and the Cherries winger stole in and smashed his finish under Petr Cech to win the game.

Jordon's goal trail was up and running and he soon scored his second goal for us in the win against West Brom!

AFC Bournemouth 2
Arsenal 1   **January 14th 2018**

CHERRIES'
MEMORABLE MOMENTS

JOSHUA KING SCORING THE WINNER VERSUS MAN UTD

I obviously played for Manchester United under Sir Alex Ferguson, he was probably one of the best managers in the world and I have nothing bad to say about him.

It wasn't a personal thing for me really. I have never been a United fan and have never supported any team – it was a big occasion because we had beaten Manchester United, not because of me.

It was a memorable moment as we'd beaten Chelsea the week before and then beaten United, they were big results that helped us stay up that season.

DAVID BROOKS SIGNING FOR THE CHERRIES...

Sheffield United gave me the chance to play and that was the main thing. Going from youth football to men's football is a big step and that's hopefully prepared me well for stepping into the Premier League.

I remember the day I signed, it was a memorable moment, but I haven't made it – I want to train well and make an impact in games.

It's the next step of my career and I'm pleased to be here.

ASMIR BEGOVIC WINNING THE PREMIER LEAGUE WITH CHELSEA

For a squad to sacrifice themselves each and every day in training to work so hard and build up to winning the Premier League is a fantastic feeling.

To have that moment in your career is great, it's a great experience to draw from – not just the moment you win it but the season as a whole.

STEVE COOK THAT GOAL AGAINST FULHAM

That was a great night for the club, one of the best games of that memorable promotion season.

It was one of the best games I've experienced since I've been here.

The goal was really special, some people say it was a cross but it was more of a cross-shot I would say! I picked up the ball and aimed for the top corner, it flew in and was one of the best goals I've ever scored. One to be proud of!

ANDREW SURMAN SCORING AGAINST BRIGHTON LAST SEASON...

It's probably one of the biggest goals of my career, we hadn't started the season well and went 1-0 down in a crucial game.

I didn't want it to go on my right foot to be honest! I waited for the defender to commit himself and thankfully I managed to sidestep him and pick my spot. You could feel the frustration around the place and it was a tough game.

It might not be a massive moment in history but it's certainly a memorable moment for myself.

PAST, PRESENT & FUTURE

WITH JUNIOR STANISLAS

PAST

FIRST REPLICA KIT...

Well, back in the day I was a Liverpool fan, that was about 20 years ago. So my first kit was a Liverpool one, no name and number, we could hardly afford the kit let alone having the name on the back!

FIRST PAIR OF BOOTS...

I had some Hi-Tec black and purple boots. I wouldn't wear them today! But I did get a hat-trick in my first game wearing them!

FIRST FOOTBALLING HERO...

Ronaldo. The best one.

FIRST RECORD BOUGHT...

Even as an eight-year-old, I liked Nas – the American rapper.

FIRST CAR...

It was a basic Vauxhall Astra.

24

WHO IS YOUR BEST MATE AT THE CLUB AND WHAT IS THEIR ANNOYING HABIT?

I've got close with most of the lads. The first person I met when I joined here was Callum Wilson, his most annoying habit is that he laughs at his own jokes all the time.

BEST LUNCH AT THE TRAINING GROUND?

That's a tough one, I'd have to say something basic like chicken and pasta – healthy!

WHO'S THE BEST CONTACT IN YOUR PHONE BOOK?

I have to say my missus as my favourite, that's a loaded question! I don't have many famous ones, I've got Draco Malfoy in my phone, one of our media officers looks like him!

WHAT MUSIC ARE YOU LISTENING TO AT THE MOMENT?

Always Meek Mill, always. I did an interview about music last year and all I said was Meek Mill!

LAST FILM YOU WATCHED?

I went to the cinema with the missus not long ago, Sicario. It was a very good film, I'd recommend it.

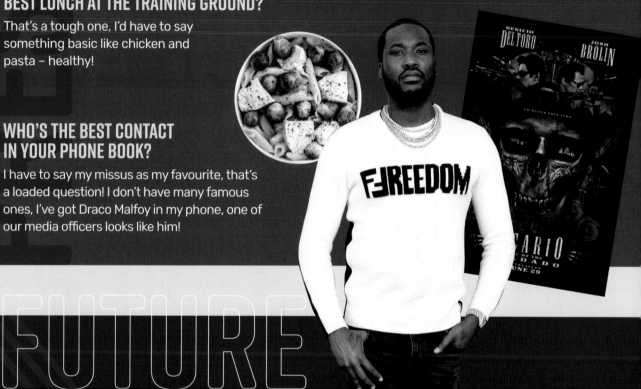

FUTURE

WILL YOU STAY IN THE GAME WHEN YOU RETIRE?

Yes, maybe as a coach. I took a session in La Manga and I've done some of my badges.

WHERE WOULD YOU LIKE TO VISIT?

New York, I'd love to go there.

WHAT GROUND WOULD YOU LIKE TO PLAY AT?

Real Madrid's Bernabéu.

WHAT HOBBY WOULD YOU LIKE TO GET MORE INTO WHEN YOU RETIRE?

I don't play golf but I have potential I think!

DO YOU HAVE AN AMBITION THAT YOU WANT TO ACHIEVE IN THE FUTURE?

I'm not really sure yet, I have lots of ambition but I'll probably start thinking about it in a few years maybe.

WHAT SPORTING EVENT WOULD YOU MOST LIKE TO GO TO?

The World Cup final – that'd be the best event.

A DAY IN THE LIFE

OF A NEW SIGNING

GORGEOUS

When a new player signs for AFC Bournemouth, fans across the world go to social media and afcb.co.uk to see how they are unveiled and what the new recruit has to say.

But what goes on behind the scenes?

Our three new summer signings Diego Rico, Jefferson Lerma and David Brooks help illustrate the process...

All of our new signings are excited to come to Vitality Stadium and after they arrive, the first thing they usually do is get examined by our medical team.

This ranges from simple exercises to seeing how far they can stretch, to having their legs measured!

This is all for the medics to use their expertise just to double-check that the player is in full health arriving at the club.

STEP 2 MEET THE CEO

The first part of the medical usually takes an hour, after that they'll remain in their training wear, head upstairs and meet the chief executive Neill Blake.

They'll more than likely sign the paperwork and finalise the transfer, that's probably the most important thing!

STEP 3 POSE FOR A PHOTO!

It's the infamous signing shot, sometimes the media team will ask for both Neill and the new player to pose with a shirt, a ball, a scarf or maybe with the contract itself. It's almost the rubber stamp photo to confirm to the world he's in the building - traditional!

STEP 4 THE TOUR

Whether it's the chief executive or manager Eddie Howe giving the tour, the new signing will get taken over to the training complex and given a tour of their new home!

The manager was on hand to give Diego a look around, with an interpreter on hand at the time to make sure Diego could fully understand.

STEP 5 ANOTHER PHOTO SHOOT

This time, with the manager. The club's media team like to get a shot of the signing with the manager, it's Eddie who wants him to be a part of the squad after all!

The player will often then walk back around to the stadium for more photos on their own, or stick around the training pavillion to do them on the nice backdrops!

STEP 6 THE INTERVIEW!

They've signed the contract, so you all want to hear why they've joined, right!? The media team will have a camera set up, usually in the press conference room at the stadium, and the player will get mic'ed up and asked a few questions.

There's a lot to say, and with Diego and Jefferson, an interpreter was on hand to ensure the correct questions were put to the pair. Depending on what stage of the season it is, the new signing may then be asked to go to a green screen, and film some celebrations for their goal GIFs, or for part of a reveal video!

STEP 7 GO HOME

We've made it seven simple steps, but it's a long day for a new player when they first join the club. There's a lot of media and introductions to be made, but as one big family it's a great start for them.

Here's to the future, lads!

MEMORABLE MOMENTS

CALLUM WILSON SCORING THE HAT-TRICK AGAINST HUDDERSFIELD AFTER HIS LONG TERM INJURY...

I was delighted to get it, that game in particular – we were two goals up and down to ten men and our backs were against the wall so I didn't think it was going to come.

It was a moment for my family, when you go through rehab it's tough but your family are there to pick you up every day.

I remember it was great for me to celebrate with the fans too who had supported me during my injury – a real highlight for me.

SIMON FRANCIS BEING HANDED THE CAPTAINCY...

I was delighted to be made permanent captain. I remember in our first season in the Premier League, I had to take the mantle in Tommy Elphick's absence and I loved every minute of it.

It was a huge step for me, when I was appointed Tommy had left the club and I spoke to him about the role and how important it was.

I love captaining the side, it's a great honour.

MARC PUGH SCORING A GOAL AGAINST BOLTON TO HELP SECURE PROMOTION...

What a night that was against Bolton. We knew we had a good chance of securing promotion and we knew what we had to do under the lights at Vitality Stadium.

I remember the goal as I cut inside and hit it with my left-foot, I did the knee slide in all the emotion and it's a goal that will stick with me for the rest of my life for sure.

DAN GOSLING SCORING A LAST MINUTE WINNER IN THE MERSEYSIDE DERBY...

I had some great moments in the FA Cup – it was a fourth round replay and in the last minute of extra time, so I don't think you could write a better script than that.

I didn't really know the magnitude of it at the time, until a couple of the lads said I'd go down in the history of the club and still to this day, I get Scousers that come up to me and thank me for that goal.

It's a great memory and probably one of the best I've had in my career.

JERMAIN DEFOE WALKING OUT AT WEMBLEY STADIUM WITH BRADLEY LOWERY...

What a great day that was – I scored against Lithuania in my first England game since 2013 and it was an unbelievable feeling.

I also got to walk out that day with Bradley and I'm blessed to be in a position where I can make someone feel that way.

People say football's just a game. I've been lucky enough to have this gift and doing something I love, and touching so many lives, little kids that are ill.

To walk out with Bradley was an honour that day.

TOP 5

WITH RYAN FRASER

With increasing responsibility, Ryan Fraser has not only become a huge fans' favourite, but one of the Premier League's most feared wingers.

His trademark direct, pacey style has been developed over time - but how has the young Scot honed his game?

Here are five of Weeman's best games throughout his career!

A NEW BEGINNING

When you go to a new club, you want to make an instant impression, and that's exactly what Ryan did when he joined Ipswich Town on loan.

Ryan often points to his loan spell at Portman Road for giving him the confidence to go on to become the player he is today – and it started at Griffin Park in the first game of the season in 2015/16.

The former Aberdeen man played a part in the first goal of the day, when he cut inside from the right and walloped a shot against the post, allowing Kevin Bru to tap in.

Ryan then made it 2-0 by tapping in inside the area – his fifth goal in the second tier.

It was a hugely impressive display, but the only negative for the Scot was the result.

He came off after 78 minutes, but Brentford equalised in the 92nd and 96th minutes and Andre Gray and England international James Tarkowski both scored.

A crazy game – but one which set up a fantastic season for Ryan!

Brentford 2
Ipswich 2
August 8th 2015

ANNOUNCING YOURSELF TO THE WORLD

AFC Bournemouth 4
Liverpool 3
December 4th 2016

The fans hadn't seen a lot of the Scottish winger in the top flight, but he put his stamp on a Premier League epic.

It truly was a game for the ages, as Liverpool raced into a two goal lead to silence the home crowd.

It seemed a comeback would be impossible against Jurgen Klopp's side, but Ryan gave the side a glimmer of hope after coming on in the 55th minute.

Seconds later, he won a penalty after being brought down by James Milner – Callum Wilson converted and that moment gave the place a lift.

Emre Can made it 3-1, but Ryan wasn't done. His first Premier League goal came to make it 3-2 with a brilliant 20-yard curling effort.

A goal and a penalty win, you'd be pleased with that right!? But Ryan was a constant threat and provided another massive moment in the match.

Jack Wilshere gave him the ball out wide and he swung in a brilliant cross for the left - Steve Cook scored a brilliant goal but Ryan's cross was sublime.

A FEIRY INTERNATIONAL DERBY

Whenever England play Scotland, it's always a feisty occasion and this game was no different, in an intense Hampden Park the passion of the game was there for all to see.

Alex Oxlade-Chamberlain fired the Three Lions into the lead, before Ryan came on for his first ever international cap.

It then became an atmosphere Ryan would never forget as three goals were scored in the last three minutes of the game!

Leigh Griffiths scored a tremendous free-kick and Hampden was bouncing as the Scots drew level.

But then Griffiths stepped up again to score another world class free-kick and the stadium felt like it was going to collapse – how intense the Scottish fans were!

It was almost a famous win for Weeman to be involved in and the first win over England since 1999, but Harry Kane scored in the 93rd minute to salvage a point in World Cup qualifying.

What a game to make your debut for your country in! One Ryan won't forget that's for sure!

Scotland 2
England 2   June 10th 2017

TOFFEE BRACE

With his influence continuing to grow in the Cherries camp, Ryan once again proved his Premier League class against Merseyside opposition.

After a slick counter-attack and quality ball across from Joshua King, Ryan was in space in the penalty area. Instead of panicking and smashing one over the bar, he composed himself and off the floor, acrobatically found the back of the net with a stunning finish.

Vitality Stadium was on its feet for the popular winger, but they were silenced when Idrissa Gueye scored against the run of play in the second half.

Sitting in the bottom three and on a poor run, we desperately needed three points. Ryan took the responsibility.

In the 90th minute, he took the ball on the left hand side, cut inside and smashed a shot which took a deflection and flew into the net!

It was a huge relief and was a match winning moment – that was our first win which not only moved us up to 14th, but started a big run of results that changed our season.

AFC Bournemouth 2   Everton 1
December 30th 2017

SURVIVAL SPECIALIST

In the latter part of the 2017/18 season, Ryan really proved how valuable being a team player really is.

With our Premier League survival needing to be 100% secured, Swansea headed to Vitality Stadium desperate for points themselves to get out of the bottom three.

It was a game where one moment would prove the difference, and Ryan once again proved that hard work does pay off with another industrious display from right-back.

In a tight game, you felt one moment of magic would win the game – and that came from a clever free-kick. Andrew Surman fooled everyone by rolling the ball to Fraser in the area and he curled a magnificent effort into the corner of the net.

It was a huge goal which capped off another tireless display from Fraser and capped off a season where he proved his value and his versatility.

AFC Bournemouth 1
Swansea 0

May 5th 2018

TRAINING TIPS

SIMON FRANCIS ON BEING A LEADER FOR THE TEAM...

It can take a while to come naturally, but leading isn't all about shouting and motivating the players with words. Actions have bigger impacts.

If you are professional every day, do all the right things from application in training to diet – then you earn respect for that and become a role model for your team mates.

Everyone is like that here in the squad, every single player works extremely hard every day and lives a professional lifestyle.

DAN GOSLING ON SCORING GOALS FROM MIDFIELD...

I always say that people should watch clips of Frank Lampard, who was one of the best midfielders in the world when he was playing and he was able to ghost into the penalty area and score plenty of goals.

I'd say you have to be very fit, as you may need to make a late run into the area and explode past someone in front of you or who is marking you – it may not always fall for you but you have to be fit and mentally prepared to keep running into the penalty area to help the strikers.

It takes time to practise, but as a midfielder it's also good to be able to shoot from distance too.

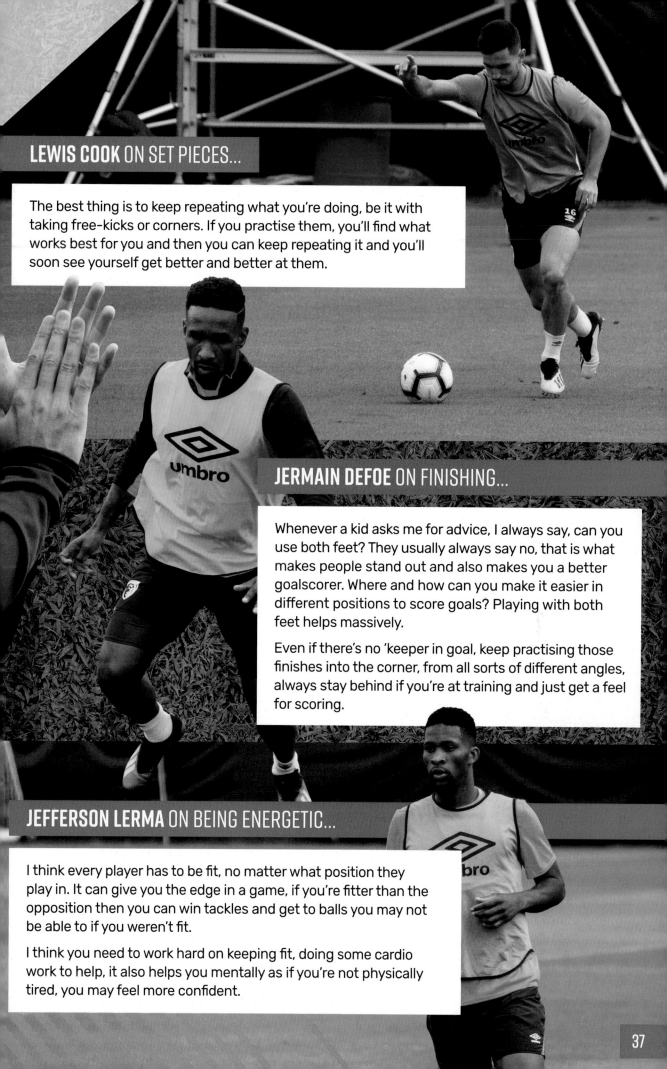

LEWIS COOK ON SET PIECES...

The best thing is to keep repeating what you're doing, be it with taking free-kicks or corners. If you practise them, you'll find what works best for you and then you can keep repeating it and you'll soon see yourself get better and better at them.

JERMAIN DEFOE ON FINISHING...

Whenever a kid asks me for advice, I always say, can you use both feet? They usually always say no, that is what makes people stand out and also makes you a better goalscorer. Where and how can you make it easier in different positions to score goals? Playing with both feet helps massively.

Even if there's no 'keeper in goal, keep practising those finishes into the corner, from all sorts of different angles, always stay behind if you're at training and just get a feel for scoring.

JEFFERSON LERMA ON BEING ENERGETIC...

I think every player has to be fit, no matter what position they play in. It can give you the edge in a game, if you're fitter than the opposition then you can win tackles and get to balls you may not be able to if you weren't fit.

I think you need to work hard on keeping fit, doing some cardio work to help, it also helps you mentally as if you're not physically tired, you may feel more confident.

GAME CHANGERS
TOP 5
WITH JERMAIN DEFOE

For nearly 20 years Jermain Defoe has been banging in the goals for club and country, including loads for the Cherries over his two spells with us.

Here are five of Jermain's big moments picked out, from scoring World Cup-winning goals, five in a Premier League match and, of course, setting the record with the Cherries while on loan with the club as a teenager.

HE SCORED TEN IN A ROW

Whenever Jermain plays for the Cherries, even today, you're bound to hear the song "We've got Jermain Defoe, he scored ten in a row", and that's all due to his amazing feat while he was with the club as a teenager.

Jermain came to Dean Court on loan in 2000 to gain experience, and he made an instant impact, scoring on his debut away at Stoke. Then he scored in his second game, then his third, he even netted two in his fourth Cherries game!

The goals kept on coming, and in his tenth league game he had the chance to equal the post-war record for the most consecutive league games scored in.

It wasn't going to be easy though as the match was away to Cambridge United, who were level on points with the Cherries, and the task became even harder when Wade Elliott was sent off for the visitors after half an hour.

But then, in the 64th minute, history was made.

Steve Fletcher and Carl Fletcher linked up and suddenly Jermain was in. He still had the 'keeper to beat, but in a flash he skipped to his left and buried the ball into the empty net. Jermain had the record – and then all of his team mates on top of him for some wild celebrations!

Cambridge United 0
AFC Bournemouth 2

January 23rd 2001

Ipswich Town 2
West Ham United 3

October 28th 2001

TOP-FLIGHT FIRST

A season later and Jermain was making tracks in the Premier League back with West Ham, and his talent on the top stage was put beyond doubt when he scored his first top-flight goal away at Ipswich.

Jermain came off the bench in the 88th minute with the score 2-1 to his side, but he still had enough time to net his maiden goal after finishing off a through ball from team mate Michael Carrick.

Ex-Cherries skipper Matt Holland pulled one back for the Tractor Boys in injury time, but Jermain's goal turned out to be the winner, and the Hammer's first away win of that season.

As had happened the season before at Dean Court, Jermain was now on a scoring run, and he finished top scorer for the Hammers that season, scoring 14 goals in total.

One of the 14 came in a 1-0 win against Manchester United at Old Trafford, and West Ham finished the season in an impressive seventh place.

SCORING A WORLD CUP WINNER

Jermain's netted 20 goals for the Three Lions, but none were more important than this one, the only goal of the game to see his country through the group stage at the World Cup in South Africa.

England had drawn with the US and Algeria in their first two games and that meant three points were needed against Slovenia in their final match, or the tournament might come to a premature end for Fabio Capello's squad.

Jermain had come off the bench in the game before but started for the first time in the tournament against Slovenia, and the striker showed it was a wise selection.

On 23 minutes James Milner's wonderful curling cross was met sweetly on the volley by Jermain and from seven yards there was nothing the Slovenia 'keeper could do to keep it out.

England were in front and the slender lead would be held until the full-time whistle.

The win sent England through, setting up an encounter with Germany in the knockout stages.

Slovenia 0
England 1   June 23rd 2010

GIMMIE FIVE!

Jermain always was an ace goalscorer for Spurs, over his two spells with the club he notched an impressive 143 goals, and on one November afternoon he managed to score a famous five in just one match!

Surprisingly, at half-time at White Hart Lane the home side only led 1-0 and Jermain had been quiet up to that point, but everything was about to change.

Bang, bang, bang! Jermain scored three goals in seven minutes and he was on his way with one of the Premier League's fastest ever hat-tricks, but there was still much more to come.

Ten minutes later Jermain bagged again with a crisp right footer and 20 minutes after that he was played through and kept his cool to become just the third player to score five in a Premier League game – and he remains the only person to date to score them all in one half! High five Jermain!

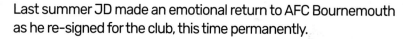

Tottenham Hotspur 9
Wigan Athletic 1   November 22nd 2009

BACK WITH A BANG

Last summer JD made an emotional return to AFC Bournemouth as he re-signed for the club, this time permanently.

After four Premier League games without a goal, the club were still searching for their first point and Jermain was still hunting down his first goal.

Newly promoted Brighton were up next at Vitality and when Solly March gave the away team the lead it looked like they might be taking them back along the coast.

But the Cherries weren't done yet! Andrew Surman drew the side level and with 73 minutes on the clock Jermain was the man on the spot to win the game.

Jordon Ibe played a clever ball through and in an instant Jermain had turned and slotted home a dart of a finish to claim three precious points in front of the adoring home supporters.

The goal had taken a while to come – it was Jermain's first Bournemouth goal in 5,977 days – but it was certainly worth the wait!

AFC Bournemouth 2
Brighton & Hove Albion 1   September 15th 2017

PAST, PRESENT & FUTURE

WITH STEVE COOK

PAST

FIRST REPLICA KIT...

It was a Liverpool one, I couldn't tell you what year though! I'm guessing late 90s, I was a fan back then.

FIRST PAIR OF BOOTS...

I had a pair of Puma Kings, they were proper classic black ones.

FIRST FOOTBALLING HERO...

Michael Owen for some reason! I just liked him, he was a big player – I liked Liverpool at the time so that probably helped. But he was an amazing player, so talented.

FIRST RECORD BOUGHT...

I'm not sure about bought, I used to download my music off Limewire, I'm not sure if that's illegal! I think it is, so sorry for that! But I'm going to guess that it was a song by Ne-yo called So Sick. It could be a lot worse!

FIRST CAR...

It was a Fiat Punto, it was black but I didn't have it long. I wrote it off unfortunately, on the way to training when I was at Brighton. Not good!

WHO IS YOUR BEST MATE AT THE CLUB AND WHAT IS THEIR ANNOYING HABIT?

I think I get on with Goso or Surs the best. Goso is annoying as I have to order him clothes online... but he always sends them back! It's a right pain!

BEST LUNCH AT THE TRAINING GROUND?

The chefs are very good you know – I'd say their spaghetti bolognese; the garlic bread is top notch and it's very healthy too!

WORST THING ABOUT TRAINING?

Hmmmm... Well as a defender I have to say finishing. It's a nightmare!

WHO'S THE BEST CONTACT IN YOUR PHONE BOOK?

Well, I'd say the best is my Mom! But the most famous is probably Jack Wilshere.

WHAT MUSIC ARE YOU LISTENING TO AT THE MOMENT?

I do like a bit of everything really, but Queen are my go-to at the moment. Not a particular song or album, just the greatest hits really. I love that, I like a lot of old school music.

WHAT TV SERIES ARE YOU INTO AT THE MOMENT?

There's two at the moment really, The Sinner and Westworld. Westworld is very, very good. If you're reading this and haven't watched it, I'd strongly recommend it.

FUTURE

WILL YOU STAY IN THE GAME WHEN YOU RETIRE?

I'd like to think so, I'm just not sure on what role really. But we'll see, hopefully yes.

WHERE WOULD YOU LIKE TO VISIT?

I'd say somewhere in Asia, maybe Japan or China. It would obviously be a very different experience to your usual holiday or whatever, it'd be great to experience their culture and see how different it is.

WHAT SPORTING EVENT WOULD YOU MOST LIKE TO GO TO?

I'd love to go to any sort of major final in football. Outside of football though, I'd love to go and watch the T20 with my friends, it's something I've wanted to do.

WHAT HOBBY WOULD YOU LIKE TO GET MORE INTO WHEN YOU RETIRE?

Well I play a little bit of golf – if I get more spare time I'd love to get better at that.

WHAT GROUND WOULD YOU LIKE TO PLAY AT?

Probably the Bernabéu – it's got such a history. I've visited before but would absolutely love to play there.

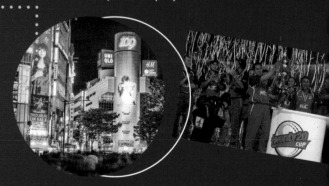

DO YOU HAVE AN AMBITION THAT YOU WANT TO ACHIEVE IN THE FUTURE?

Well I passed my B License in my coaching badges and I'd probably like to go to the next level on that side of things.

TRAINING TIPS

CHARLIE DANIELS ON SCORING FROM DISTANCE...

It's a good weapon for any player on the pitch to have, I scored the goal against Manchester City, but to be honest, I'd never struck one like that before!

I've scored a few from range in my career and it's all about keeping your head over the ball. Don't lean back as you'll probably blast it over, keep your head over the ball and keep practising them on the training pitches.

LYS MOUSSET ON DRIBBLING PAST PLAYERS...

I think having quick feet helps. Work on your foot speed and it can get you out of some difficult situations. Watching tricks on YouTube can also help, then you can recreate them yourself.

I think you also need to look at the defender's body shape, if they're leaning to one side, it might give you an opportunity to dribble on the other side. It's not easy but keep practising and get those feet moving!

JOSHUA KING ON BEING AN ALL-ROUND CENTRE FORWARD...

I think you always have to expect the worst from a defender – they are the last line before the goalkeeper so you always have to think how you can get in and score goals.

Finishing is always key for a striker, but sometimes it's not all about goals – but how hard you work for the team. You could press a defender and he could give the ball away to a team mate.

In this team we always work hard for the team before getting goals for ourselves and I think that's important.

ANDREW SURMAN ON KEEPING CALM WHEN THINGS AREN'T GOING WELL...

That's really important, particularly at the top level when teams can punish you in an instant.

If you go a goal down, you never know what can happen – a lot can turn around in five minutes let alone fifty!

It comes with experience but you can't lose your head, if you keep your head you could catch out an opponent who has just scored. You have to believe in yourself that you can make a difference.

Sometimes it may be keeping the ball after some pressure, or you're losing and need to get back into the game, but you have to believe in yourself and your team mates no matter what the situation.

45

TOP 5

WITH LEWIS COOK

A World Cup winner, senior England international and Premier League regular. Not bad all by the age of 21!

Having been born in Leeds and rising through the ranks at Elland Road, Lewis Cook joined AFC Bournemouth as one of the country's brightest talents in 2015.

His star has only continued to shine on the south coast, and in the summer he committed his future to the club by signing a four-year deal.

Here are five of the standout games of Lewis' career, for many different reasons!

A mixed day for Lewis, but an unforgettable game for sure! Leeds United opened the 2014/15 season away to Millwall, having finished 15th the previous season and under new manager Dave Hockaday.

Their top scorer Ross McCormack, who scored 29 goals, was sold to Fulham and 14 other first-team squad members also left the club. But this presented an opportunity for Lewis – with the team 1-0 down – he came on after the hour mark for his senior debut.

Aged just 17, he was thrust into the Championship, but a proud day became a mixed one when he gave away a penalty and Millwall scored to make it 2-0!

Making your debut aged 17 would be a huge achievement, but to do so for your boyhood club in England's second tier adds to the accomplishment. It was the day that Lewis came onto the nation's radar and he hasn't looked back since!

Millwall 2
Leeds United 0

August 9th 2014

MAKING A STATEMENT

After a season hampered by injury, Lewis probably didn't play as much as he'd have liked in his first season with the Cherries. But in a big game against Middlesbrough at Vitality Stadium, it was time for Lewis to shine.

The Cherries headed into the game without a win in four, prompting the critics to suggest they could be dragged into the relegation battle. But the Cherries were in rampant form.

When Dan Gosling had to be replaced a minute before half-time, Lewis came on and gave the home fans a performance to suggest that he was capable of becoming the lynchpin of the team.

He registered his first Premier League assist in the second-half – picking the ball up from deep, Lewis sprayed a magnificent first-time pass right through the Boro defence which Marc Pugh did excellently to convert.

AFC Bournemouth 4
Middlesbrough 0

April 22nd 2017

WORLD CUP WINNING CAPTAIN

Korea was the setting for one of Lewis' finest moments in his young career so far.

He became the first man to lift a World Cup for England since Bobby Moore lifted the Jules Rimet trophy in 1966, after captaining England under-20s in the Under-20 FIFA World Cup final.

In a tense final against Venezuela in Suwon, a first-half strike from Dominic Calvert-Lewin put the Three Lions ahead.

Newcastle United's Freddie Woodman then saved a second-half penalty, with Lewis dominating the game and being a real talisman for the side.

The final win wasn't just inspiring for those under-20s players though, as it was the first success of a memorable summer for English football.

It started a chain reaction of successes, with England's youth sides winning the under-17s European Championship, the Toulon Tournament, the European Under-19 Championship and the Under-17 World Cup.

More than just a cup final for Lewis to cap off a tournament and begin a summer of success!

Venezuela U20 0
England U20 1   11th June 2017

THE BEGINNING TO LIFE AS A REGULAR

A 0-0 draw with Leicester City at the start of the season won't be best remembered by the fans, only really for us missing chances to win the game – but hear us out!

It was the first start of the 2017/18 season in the Premier League for Lewis and it looked as though his learning process from the previous season had well and truly sunk in.

He bossed the game from start to finish, winning man of the match in a physical battle against serial Europa League winner Vincente Iborra and powerhouse Wilfred Ndidi.

If the Middlesbrough game the season before opened supporters' eyes to Lewis' potential, this one definitely made them stand up and take notice.

It was the start of a remarkable season for Lewis who would then go on to break into the team as a 20-year-old and keep his place for the campaign.

AFC Bournemouth 0
Leicester City 0

September 30th 2017

ENGLAND DEBUT

England 1
Italy 1
March 27th 2018

Simply an historic day for the football club! Lewis became the first ever serving AFC Bournemouth player to make his full international debut for England.

It looked like the midfielder wasn't going to come on as he warmed up on the touchline at the famous Wembley Stadium, with plenty of established internationals and Premier League talents surrounding him.

But with 19 minutes to go, Gareth Southgate beckoned for Cook and wanted him to play a part against a strong Italy side.

In a tight game, which Jamie Vardy had given the Three Lions the lead in, Cook replaced Jesse Lingard and did not look out of place against the likes of Jorginho, Lorenzo Insigne and Marco Parolo.

The game finished in a 1-1 draw as the Azzurri scored late on, but the result was insignificant as Lewis' hard work over the season earned him one of the highest honours in football.

49

PAST, PRESENT & FUTURE

WITH TYRONE MINGS

PAST

FIRST REPLICA KIT...

A Liverpool shirt, I had Collymore on the back of it. It had a big round collar and was a huge shirt, it was quite nice actually!

FIRST PAIR OF BOOTS...

A pair of red Puma Kings.

FIRST FOOTBALLING HERO...

Steven Gerrard. I always wanted to play against him, he went to the MLS the year I signed for Bournemouth so I was gutted about that. He was a big hero back in the day.

FIRST RECORD BOUGHT...

Probably something illegal off Limewire! My music knowledge wasn't vast back then so probably something like Nelly, maybe his song Grillz!

FIRST CAR...

A green Citroen Saxo with white wheels – you can probably guess that it was horrendous!

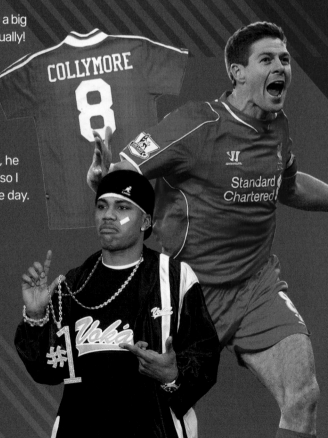

WHO IS YOUR BEST MATE AT THE CLUB AND WHAT IS THEIR ANNOYING HABIT?

Joshua King. Sometimes he forgets to say please and it winds me up, he claims it's because English is his second language but it annoys me!

BEST LUNCH AT THE TRAINING GROUND?

We have a good spaghetti bolognese.

WORST THING ABOUT TRAINING?

Running.

WHO'S THE BEST CONTACT IN YOUR PHONE BOOK?

My dad. It's boring I know but it's who I speak to the most!

WHAT MUSIC ARE YOU LISTENING TO AT THE MOMENT?

Well I've moved on from Nelly to something more cultured! I genuinely listen to Smooth Radio at the moment.

LAST FILM YOU WATCHED?

I can't really remember, I don't really watch Netflix, maybe it was something on a plane... Oh I know! It was The Big Short, it's a good film about a Wall Street kind of thing - a group of investors bet against the US mortgage market.

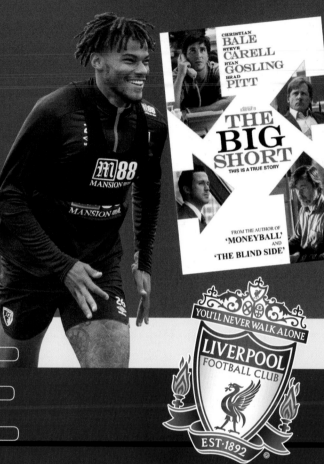

FUTURE

WILL YOU STAY IN THE GAME WHEN YOU RETIRE?

Yeah, but not as a coach. I want to be in the boardroom as an agent or CEO.

WHERE WOULD YOU LIKE TO VISIT?

I would love to go to Singapore, that would be great.

WHAT SPORTING EVENT WOULD YOU MOST LIKE TO GO TO?

The Superbowl.

WHAT GROUND WOULD YOU LIKE TO PLAY AT?

Anfield, I've unfortunately not played there yet, I've visited before but would absolutely love to play there.

WHAT HOBBY WOULD YOU LIKE TO GET MORE INTO WHEN YOU RETIRE?

I think playing a musical instrument – I don't have anything in mind at the moment. The piano maybe, the manager's doing that now.

DO YOU HAVE AN AMBITION THAT YOU WANT TO ACHIEVE IN THE FUTURE?

Not really in business or anything, I think once I'm done playing I want to be content and happy with what I've achieved in the game. That would be the biggest thing for me, I want to do well.

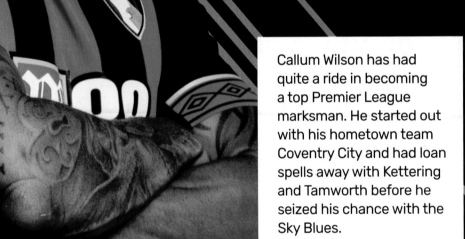

TOP 5

WITH **CALLUM WILSON**

Callum Wilson has had quite a ride in becoming a top Premier League marksman. He started out with his hometown team Coventry City and had loan spells away with Kettering and Tamworth before he seized his chance with the Sky Blues.

Loads of goals later and the Cherries swooped for the talented striker and brought him to Vitality Stadium.

Championship promotion, goals galore and a Premier League hat-trick, Callum was in dreamland, only for serious knee injury to strike, twice!

Plenty of rehab later and Callum's now back to his best and banging in the goals like he's never been away!

UP AND COMING CALLUM

Callum was a bit of a late bloomer with Coventry but his unbelievable form in his first full season with the Sky Blues paved the way for him to make it to the top with the Cherries.

The campaign was a tough one for Coventry, financial problems meant they started the season with a ten-point penalty and this was their first 'home' game played at Northampton Town's stadium, but Wilson helped to make sure their housewarming party was a good one, scoring twice in a thriller.

Wilson scored as the home team went 3-0 up, but it was 3-3 with 15 minutes to go after a Bristol fightback, only for Wilson to score his second and restore the lead. It was soon 4-4 before Coventry scored a late winner.

Callum had only scored once for the Sky Blues before that season, but he scored 22 over the campaign and won the player of the year award.

Those on the south coast had been watching Callum's progress, and he was signed up that summer for his first shot at the Championship with the Cherries!

Coventry City 5
Bristol City 4
April 27th 2015

CHAMPIONSHIP CHERRY

A new club, a new season, was Callum overawed ahead of his first match in the Championship with Bournemouth? Not a bit of it!

Callum started the game for the away team and quickly showed the travelling Cherries fans just how talented he was.

First, he sprinted onto a through ball and beat the 'keeper with a precise finish, and after the break he latched onto a cross to steer home a volley, what a debut!

A great day almost became a perfect one, Callum had the chance to score a hat-trick in his very first Cherries game after he won his side a penalty – but it wasn't to be as the 'keeper saved the spot kick.

The performance was just the start of another amazing season for Callum and his team mates!

Huddersfield Town 0   AFC Bournemouth 4 | August 9th 2014

WE ARE GOING UP

Fast forward eight months and what a year it had been for Callum. He had over 20 goals already with two games to go, and if he could help the Cherries beat Bolton they would be promoted to the Premier League for the first time.
The Bolton defenders must have known that stopping Callum was going to be a difficult task, but they managed to keep him wrapped up for 78 minutes – the problem was that the Cherries were in such good form that Marc Pugh and Matt Ritchie already had them two goals up by then!

Callum wanted to join the goalscoring party though, and he soon did just that. The ball was played low into the box and his first touch was perfect, turning him around his marker and giving him the space to stab into the net, 3-0 and the Cherries were going up!

With 23 goals, Callum was the club's top scorer, he was "Bournemouth's goal machine", and now the team would be rubbing shoulders with the big guns of the Premier League!

AFC Bournemouth 3
Bolton Wanderers 0

April 27th 2015

WELCOME TO THE TOP FLIGHT

Could the Cherries survive in the Premier League, and could Callum make another step up? We'd lost our first two games 1-0 and West Ham away was the next tough task.

Swish! Callum struck to turn home Simon Francis' cross and he and the Cherries had their first top-flight goal.

Flash! Callum pounced on a defensive lapse and buried his finish past the 'keeper to give the visitors breathing space.

Slide! Callum places home his penalty after Max Gradel was fouled in the box – the Cherries were on their way to their first Premier League points and Callum had scored a hat-trick!

The striker scored two more in his next three games, now it was time for Premier League to learn about our goal machine!

West Ham United 3
AFC Bournemouth 4   August 22nd 2015

BACK WITH A BANG

After his stunning start to life in the Premier League, serious injury struck not just once but twice for Callum, leaving him on the sidelines for two long spells as he recovered from two knee surgeries.

Last autumn Wilson announced his return with a goal in his first game back against Middlesbrough in the Carabao Cup, and any fitness doubts were put to bed with another hat-trick as he again proved to be a thorn in the side of the Terriers.

Within five first-half minutes Callum had headed home a corner and then swiped home a bouncing ball with his usual class, Callum was back!

Harry Arter added a third, even though the home side were reduced to ten men, and with time running out Callum slammed home another to complete his treble, collecting another match ball which he kicked high into the sky in celebration. "I was sending it to be with my other one," said the striker after the match!

QUIZ TIME

2017/18 QUICK QUIZ

1. The Cherries enjoyed another successful Premier League season, but where did the team finish?

A) 10th   **B)** 9th   **C)** 12th

....

2. True or False, Marc Pugh made his 300th Cherries appearance during the season?

....

3. Against which team did the Cherries record their biggest win of the season – Huddersfield, Swansea or Burnley?

....

4. Name the three goalscorers when the Cherries beat Chelsea 3-0 at Stamford Bridge.

....

....

....

5. Who got more assists for us in the league last season, Jordon Ibe or Andrew Surman?

....

6. How many league goals did Callum Wilson score last season in the league?

A) 6   **B)** 8   **C)** 10

....

7. What squad number did Lys Mousset wear last season?

A) 9   **B)** 29   **C)** 31

....

8. True or false, Jermain Defoe scored a goal in cup competitions for the Cherries last season?

....

WORDSEARCH

Hidden in the wordsearch below are the names of 25 AFC Bournemouth players, can you find them all? Words go horizontally, vertically, diagonally and backwards.

M	F	N	T	C	A	W	E	R	S	S	Y	P	M
R	R	A	M	R	E	L	N	G	A	Q	B	B	I
X	A	U	E	V	C	A	K	L	A	T	H	E	N
V	S	M	K	O	M	N	S	O	E	U	K	G	G
V	E	F	S	R	F	I	S	S	O	A	E	O	S
C	R	L	U	D	N	E	S	I	I	C	D	V	H
G	U	S	N	A	A	U	D	I	C	A	L	I	T
N	Q	R	T	O	O	L	X	Y	N	N	I	C	I
I	N	S	O	M	S	E	E	I	K	K	A	C	M
L	O	H	X	B	B	P	E	Z	O	I	R	R	S
S	S	Y	B	I	E	L	M	E	O	N	I	I	F
O	L	U	R	C	S	J	U	I	C	G	C	Q	J
G	I	B	R	O	O	K	S	Q	S	S	O	L	A
J	W	H	G	U	P	Z	W	R	O	L	Y	A	T

AKE	BEGOVIC	BORUC	BROOKS	DANIELS
DEFOE	FRANCIS	FRASER	GOSLING	IBE
KING	LCOOK	LERMA	MINGS	MOUSSET
PUGH	RAMSDALE	RICO	SCOOK	SIMPSON
SMITH	STANISLAS	SURMAN	TAYLOR	WILSON

Answers on Page 62.

CROSSWORD

CHERRIES

Answers on Page 62

58

DOWN

1. Back in 2016, which club did we record our biggest Premier League win over?

2. This furry friend is our mascot, you can say hello to him on matchdays.

3. He's played more times for the club than anyone else, and now he's a coach with us.

4. He is Eddie Howe's right-hand man.

5. Bournemouth's Bosnian, find him between the sticks.

6. The Cherries used to be called Bournemouth and _____ Athletic.

8. He scored ten in a row some years ago – and is now back with us!

11. He's our manager – and he used to be play for us as well.

12. The club's famous stripes are red and which other colour?

15. He played for and managed the club, before more recently managing Pompey and Spurs.

17. This is where the Cherries play their home Premier League games.

ACROSS

4. Who was our top scorer over our first three Premier League seasons?

7. This club were the Cherries' first ever opponents in the Premier League.

9. How many goals did we net against champions Chelsea when we beat them in January 2018?

10. We signed this player from Chelsea, and he was player of the season in 2017/18.

13. We were 3-1 down but secured a famous 4-3 win over which big name club in 2016?

14. Which country does our speedy winger Ryan Fraser play for?

16. This striker scored the Cherries' first ever Premier League goal, and has scored loads since too!

18. He's the club's skipper and plays in defence.

19. This player was the first ever Cherries man to win a senior England cap.

SPOT THE BALL

There are too many footballs! Can you work out which is the real ball in each photo?

BALL A

Answer: ....

BALL B

Answer: ....

NAME THE TEAM

Can you name all the players in this team photo?

1.. 2.. 3..

4.. 5.. 6..

7..

LEGENDS XI

Can you name these 11 players just from the clues we've given you?

ST1: The club's all-time record appearance holder!

....

ST2: Striker from Brittany, YK!

....

LM: Currently at Newcastle, scorer of the 2015/16 goal of the season!

....

RM: Winger, WE!

....

CM1: Our current Under 21s boss!

....

CM2: Irish international now on loan at Cardiff City this season!

....

LB: Scottish club legend who also played for Chelsea!

....

RB: Irish hard man from the 1986/87 season, TF!

....

CB1: Skipper when the club first went to Wembley in 1996.

....

CB2: Captain for some of the 2008/09 season, currently at Charlton!

....

GK: Long standing league goalkeeper, won promotion from League Two and League One!

....

QUIZ TIME

2017/18 QUICK QUIZ

1. C
2. True
3. Huddersfield (4-0)
4. Callum Wilson, Junior Stanislas, Nathan Aké
5. Jordon Ibe (6)
6. B
7. C
8. False

SPOT THE BALL

Ball A: 8

Ball B: 7

WORDSEARCH

```
M F N T C A W E R S S Y P M
R R A M R E L N G A Q B B I
X A U E V C A K L A T H E N
V S M K O M N S O E U K G G
V E F S R F I S S O A E O S
C R L U D N E S I I C D V H
G U S N A A U D I C A L I T
N Q R T O O L X Y N N I C I
I N S O M S E E I K K A C M
L O H X B B P E Z O I R R S
S S Y B I E L M E O N I I F
O L U R C S J U I C G C Q J
G I B R O O K S Q S S O L A
J W H G U P Z W R O L Y A T
```

NAME THE TEAM

1. Asmir Begovic
2. Charlie Daniels
3. Adam Smith
4. Joshua King
5. Nathan Aké
6. Dan Gosling
7. Ryan Fraser

CHERRIES CROSSWORD

Down

1. Hull City
2. Cherry Bear
3. Steve Fletcher
4. Jason Tindall
5. Asmir Begovic
6. Boscombe
8. Jermain Defoe
11. Eddie Howe
12. Black
15. Harry Redknapp
17. Vitality Stadium

Across

4. Joshua King
7. Aston Villa
9. Three
10. Nathan Aké
13. Liverpool
14. Scotland
16. Callum Wilson
18. Simon Francis
19. Lewis Cook

LEGENDS XI

GK: Shwan Jalal
CB1: Ian Cox
CB2: Jason Pearce
RB: Tommy Heffernan
LB: Warren Cummings
CM1: Carl Fletcher
CM2: Harry Arter
RM: Wade Elliot
LM: Matt Ritchie
ST1: Steve Fletcher
ST2: Yann Kermorgant

September 1992.

STITCHES
FOR
EMBROIDERY

STITCHES
FOR
EMBROIDERY

HEATHER JOYNES

Kangaroo Press

Acknowledgments

My grateful thanks for their contributions to this book to: Adrienne Allen, Marie Cavanagh, Kath Chate, Effie Mitrofanis and Julie Wicks, and especially to Doris Waltho for all her help, and to my husband Jack for his unfailing support and helpful criticism. Unless otherwise credited, the embroidery, photography and diagrams are the work of the author.

Conversion Table

Common measurements used in this book converted from metric to inches:

10 mm = 1 cm
1 cm = ⅜ inch
5 cm = 2 inches
0.5 m = 50 cm = 19¾ inches
1 metre = 39⅜ inches

First published in 1991 by Kangaroo Press Pty Ltd
3 Whitehall Road (P.O. Box 75) Kenthurst 2156
Typeset by G.T. Setters Pty Limited
Printed in Hong Kong by Colorcraft Ltd

ISBN 0 86417 371 7

CONTENTS

INTRODUCTION

This book is about using stitches effectively. It is not necessary to know a great number of stitches to be a successful embroiderer. An embroidery in only one stitch can often be much more effective than one with ten different stitches. The most difficult part of starting an embroidery is choosing a suitable stitch to begin.

Too many different stitches in one piece of work can result in a confused texture. The effect of a stitch can be altered by using different threads, changing the direction, working it evenly or unevenly, large or small.

Twenty stitches are used in this book, and all of them have been varied for different effects in different sections. If you are unfamiliar with any of the stitches illustrated in these four pages it would be helpful to practise them in an attractive colour scheme. The sampler can be made up into a useful needlecase. Two rows about 15 cm long of each stitch would look good and should be enough to ensure that you will remember the stitch.

The sections of this book include many of the most-used subjects in embroidery, providing a rich reference of ideas and starting points. Each section begins with a sampler of ideas, followed by a finished piece of work based on the theme of the section,

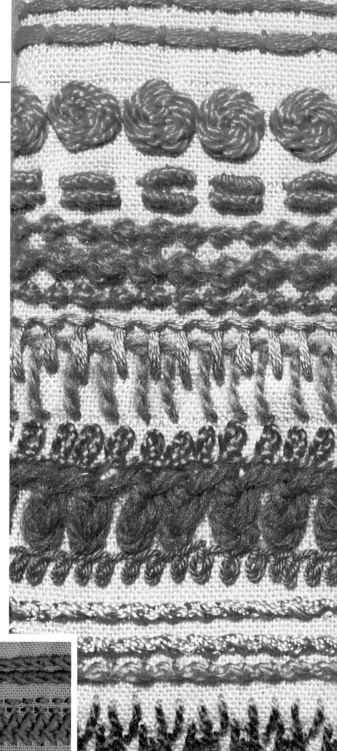

A section of a sampler.

A sampler made up as
a needlecase (11 × 15 cm)

an additional photograph and a small embroidery inspired by it. Specific details of threads and the stitch variations used in each embroidery are given so that the reader can see exactly how the effect is created.

Designing is never easy, requiring careful preparation and study of the subject to be embroidered. A design can be worked out from a drawing or a painting, from a photograph or a combination of techniques. Even if your choice of subject is a design from another book, you can add a personal touch by working in a favourite colour scheme or by changing or adding to the design to suit the format of the embroidery.

The section Getting It All Together (page 80) should be useful to newcomers to designing. Some outline designs are included in this section for those who feel happier with a readymade design.

Unless otherwise stated, the embroidery, photography and diagrams are the work of the author.

STITCH SAMPLER

The twenty stitches used in this book are all illustrated here. They are, from the top:

Portuguese stem stitch   Two rows, worked in six strands of stranded cotton.

Back stitch   Two rows, worked in perle cotton No. 8.

Herringbone stitch   One row, in perle cotton No. 5.

Alternating stem stitch   Three rows, worked in perle cotton Nos. 8 and 5.

Running stitch   Three rows, in perle cotton No. 5.

Twisted chain stitch   Two rows, in perle cotton No. 8.

Chain stitch   Two rows, in six strands of stranded cotton and shiny viscose thread.

Oyster chain stitch   One row, in tapestry wool.

Cretan stitch   Two rows, in perle cotton No. 8.

Stem stitch   Three rows, in handspun silk thread.

Straight stitch   One row, in crewel wool.

Fly stitch   Three rows, in perle cotton No. 8.

Whipped chain stitch   Three rows, in perle cotton No. 8 and viscose thread.

Rosette chain stitch   Three rows, in broder cotton, tapestry wool and perle cotton No. 8.

Buttonhole stitch   Two rows, in crewel wool and six strands of stranded cotton.

Double knot stitch   Three rows, in perle cotton No. 8, tapestry wool and crewel wool.

Bullion knot   Two rows, in perle cotton No. 8.

Spider's web: One row, in perle cotton No. 8.

Couching   Two rows, in stranded cotton.

French knots   Two rows, in perle cotton No. 5.

MATERIALS

Fabrics and threads suitable for embroidery abound today, to the point where making a choice sometimes becomes difficult. Always bear in mind the purpose of the embroidery—for instance, does it need to wash well? will it be handled continually, or worn?

The most commonly used embroidery threads are stranded cotton and perle cotton. Perle cotton comes in four thicknesses, No. 3 being the thickest, then 5, 8 and 12. The range of colours in the fine No. 12 is limited compared to the other thicknesses. Other threads of interest are viscose stranded threads, which are very shiny, velvet yarn, linen thread and Danish flower thread, which is matt. Wools include tapestry wool and crewel wool, which is a finer thread. Knitting yarns can also be used, and ribbons. Handspun wool and silk are also available at times—the uneven quality of these yarns makes for interesting textures.

Beginners will find that just purchasing materials for one project at a time means they will fairly rapidly amass a store of materials. Embroiderers are great hoarders of fabrics, threads, beads and ribbons. After a few years of stitching one can usually find materials to work on almost any project in one's stock.

Some embroidery is best worked in a frame. Various sizes and styles of embroidery hoops and frames can be obtained from good embroidery shops, where advice on the use and dressing of frames is usually available also. Two words of warning here—be careful not to pull your fabric too tight, distorting it, in a frame, and be especially careful to always work with clean hands.

The most commonly used needles for embroidery are crewel needles and tapestry needles. Crewel needles have a sharp point and long eye, tapestry needles have a blunt point and large long eye. Both are available in a large range of sizes. Always choose a needle that takes the thread easily. If the eye is too small for the thread it will be hard to pull through the fabric. The head of the needle is the widest part of it and has to make a hole in the fabric large enough for the thread to pass through.

A good pair of embroidery scissors with sharp points is essential. They should be kept for embroidery only.

A thimble is useful and worth getting used to using, as it will prevent a sore finger.

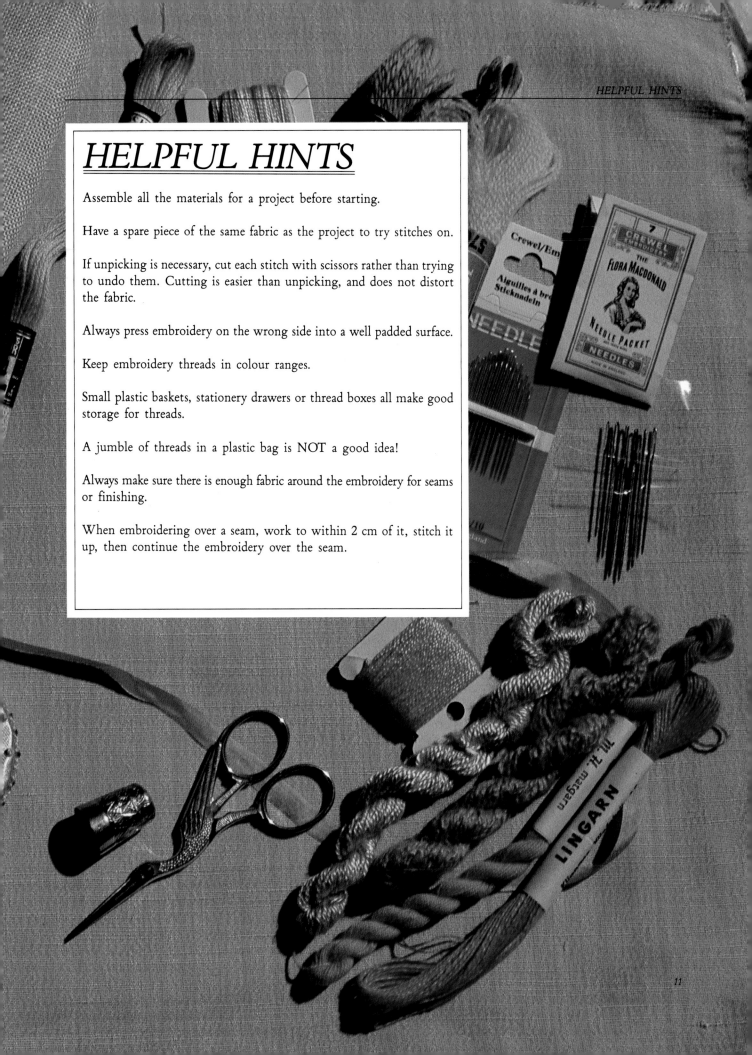

HELPFUL HINTS

Assemble all the materials for a project before starting.

Have a spare piece of the same fabric as the project to try stitches on.

If unpicking is necessary, cut each stitch with scissors rather than trying to undo them. Cutting is easier than unpicking, and does not distort the fabric.

Always press embroidery on the wrong side into a well padded surface.

Keep embroidery threads in colour ranges.

Small plastic baskets, stationery drawers or thread boxes all make good storage for threads.

A jumble of threads in a plastic bag is NOT a good idea!

Always make sure there is enough fabric around the embroidery for seams or finishing.

When embroidering over a seam, work to within 2 cm of it, stitch it up, then continue the embroidery over the seam.

THE STITCHES

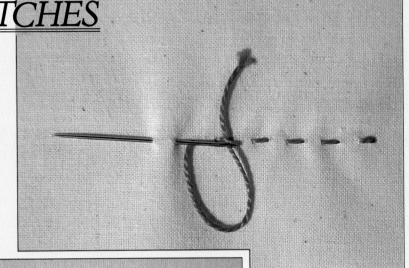

Running stitch One of the simplest stitches; very useful for achieving broken lines and light textures.

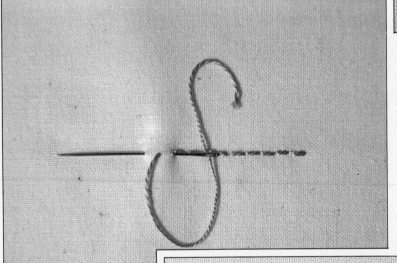

Back stitch Can make a textured line and can also be used as a filling. Single back stitches worked in all directions give a speckled effect known as seeding.

Straight stitch Extremely useful; groups of stitches can be worked to suggest plants, shadows, stems, foliage, water or parts of buildings.

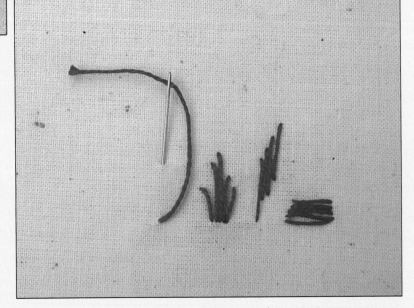

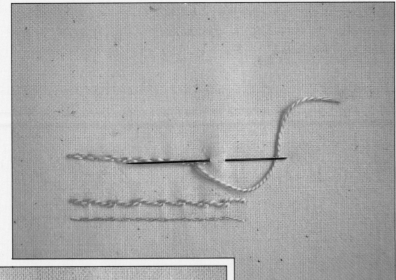

Stem stitch Unbeatable for a smooth line, but can also be worked to make a more uneven line by not making each stitch connect with the previous one. It makes a very good close filling stitch.

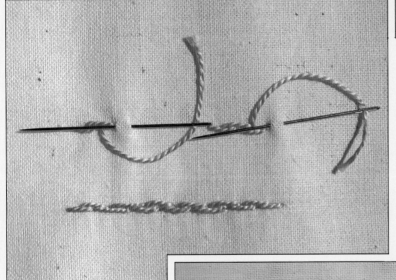

Alternating stem stitch The thread is alternately above and below the needle, resulting in a double line of stitches that can be used as a textured line or filling.

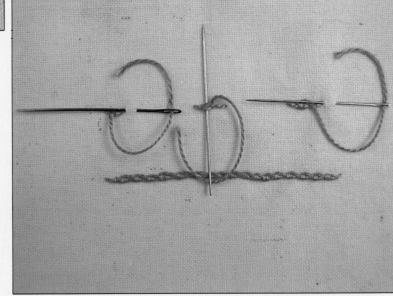

Portuguese stem stitch To start, work two stem stitches, then pass the needle under both of these twice, where they lie side by side (not through the fabric). Then work another stem stitch, repeat the two twists under it and the previous stitch, and so on.

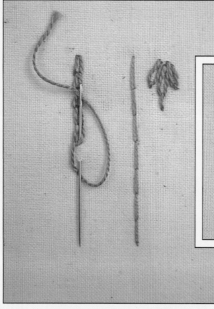

◄ *Chain stitch* Can be varied in many ways. As a line or filling the stitches can be even or uneven. Single chains can be worked as leaves or flowers. Working in a fine thread with long stitches results in a very fine line.

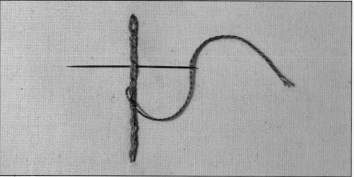

▲ *Whipped chain stitch* Makes a very firm strong line. A row of chain stitch is worked first, then every stitch is whipped with either the same thread or a different colour or weight.

Twisted chain stitch A more textured stitch. The needle is ◄ put into the fabric over the working thread instead of beside it. It makes a slightly knotty line or filling.

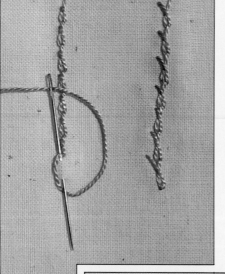

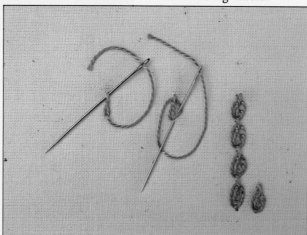

▲ *Rosette chain stitch* Worked from right to left. Start with a twisted chain, then pass the needle under the top of the stitch (not through the fabric) and make the next stitch over the working thread.

Oyster chain stitch A further development of twisted and rosette chains. Work a rosette chain, then put the needle into the loop at the right hand side of the stitch and bring it out directly under the rosette chain with the thread under the needle. Pull through and repeat. This is a very good stitch for creating texture and can be worked in a line, in rows or singly.

Fly stitch　Wonderful for making patterns and textures. It can be worked with a short or long tail, in rows side by side or one underneath the other, in groups evenly or unevenly, and in circles and curves.

Cretan stitch　A very versatile stitch as it can be worked evenly or unevenly, close or spaced apart. The stitch can also be varied by bringing the needle out close to the centre of the stitch or towards the outer edges. When working, the thread always lies to the right and the point of the needle is towards the centre of the stitch.

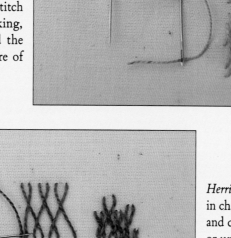

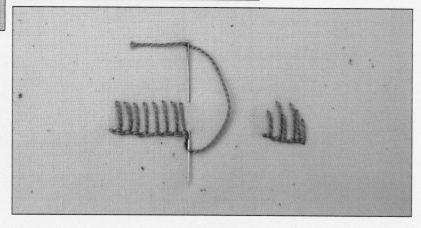

Herringbone stitch　Similar in character to Cretan stitch and can also be used evenly or unevenly, either close or spaced.

Buttonhole stitch　Can be varied by altering the length and angle of the upright part of the stitch. It takes a curve or circle well too.

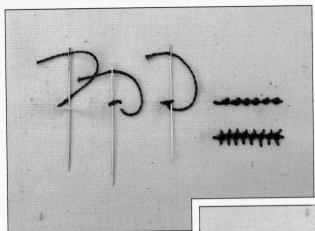

Double knot stitch Looks best in a firm twisted thread such as perle cotton. Bring the thread through and take a small stitch, bringing the needle out just underneath where it went in. Pass the needle and thread over this stitch (not through the fabric), then make a buttonhole stitch on the right side of the initial stitch; continue in the same way. A variation is to make the initial stitch larger and on a slant, pulling the knot into the centre as it is worked. This will leave part of the initial stitch extended each side of the knot.

French knot The secret of a good French knot is to wind the thread around the needle ONCE ONLY. If a larger knot is required, use double thread or thicker thread.

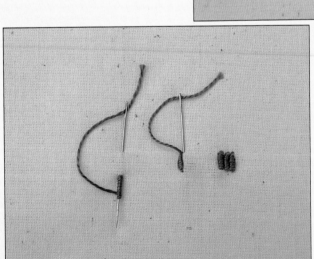

Bullion knot Bring the thread through the fabric and make a stitch the length of the knot required, bringing the needle out exactly where the thread came through initially, and taking the needle through up to the eye. Wind the thread clockwise around the needle the number of times it will take to fill the length of the knot. Hold the twists down with the left thumb while pulling the needle and thread through the fabric and twists. Tighten the working thread, pulling the knot to the right hand side of the stitch, then putting the needle through the fabric in the same place on the right of the stitch. Bullion knots take a little practice to make them fat and even.

Couching Can be worked as a single line or in a continuous line to fill a shape. The thread to be couched is brought through the fabric and held on the line to be worked with the left hand while stitching over it with either the same type of thread or a finer thread. The couching thread can be made almost invisible by slanting the stitches into the twist of the laid thread.

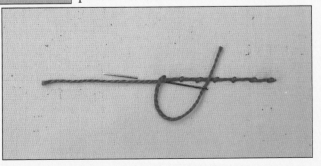

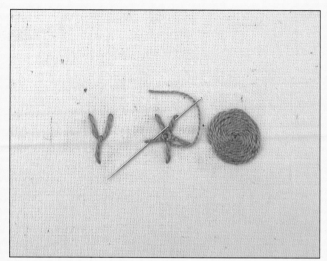

Spider's web This stitch makes lovely round spots that can be used for flowers or flower centres. The groundwork for the stitch is best worked in a firm twisted thread. For a small web, work a fly stitch, making all three legs the same length, then put a straight stitch each side, making five evenly spaced legs. Bring the needle and thread out at the centre of the groundwork and weave over and under the legs, round and round until the whole circle is filled up and the legs are covered completely. A web larger than about 1 cm in diameter will need more legs, either seven or nine—always an uneven number. The size of the groundwork will have to be adjusted accordingly.

STARTING AND FINISHING

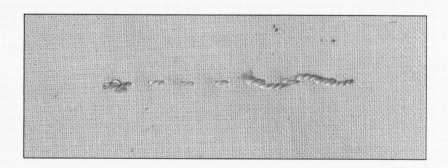

To start, make a small back stitch, then work the first stitch over it.

OR

Leave about 10 cm of thread at the back and weave it through the stitches when worked. This is best for heavy threads.

Starting with a knot is permissible as long as the thread is not too thick and the back of the work is to be lined.

LINES

Stitches can make an infinite variety of lines. They can be straight, curved, broken, heavy, fine and knotted, textured or cross hatched, just to name a few. Choosing the right stitch and thread to give the effect desired takes experience. It is important to decide on the thickness of the line to be worked before starting the stitching. This is all part of the designing and planning which is an essential part of embroidery.

1. Broken lines, from the top: Running stitch in six strands of shaded stranded cotton, with the rows bricked. Next, parallel rows of running stitch using broder cotton. Then French knots, worked in perle cotton No. 5, followed by bullion knots in perle cotton No. 8. Then back stitch in a shaded shiny rayon thread, and last, double knot stitch in a knitting yarn, worked with a space between the stitches.

2. Stem stitch cannot be surpassed for fine smooth lines and is shown here in wavy lines worked in stranded cotton, one strand at the top group of lines, followed by a group in two strands, and then three strands.

3. Another group of curved lines in varieties of chain stitch. From the left, the first three rows are worked in fine silk, making the chain stitches very long. Then broder cotton worked in a much shorter stitch. Twisted chain is next, in a shaded green rayon thread, followed by whipped chain in perle cotton No. 5. Then three rows of whipped chain in stranded cotton, using three strands, two strands, then one strand.

4. A section of heavy lines. Starting from the top, Portuguese stem stitch in six strands of stranded cotton, then crewel wool, then perle cotton No. 5. This is followed by double knot stitch in tapestry wool, then a rayon weaving yarn. The rows following are all versions of couching, starting with handspun silk thread couched with sewing cotton.

5. Lines cross hatched are handspun silk thread couched with a dark sewing cotton, overlaid with a long coarse stem stitch in perle cotton No. 5.

6. Buttonhole stitch is used for the concentric ovals, using perle cotton No. 5 at the centre, followed by crewel wool, then another colour in perle No. 5 on the outside. The lines of the stitch add to the pattern of the circular lines. Herringbone stitch in a fine silk makes a contrasting series of lines between the two outer rows of buttonhole stitch.

The background fabric is a cotton twill.

Lines (20 × 28 cm)

This panel of stitchery demonstrates the use of different threads to create contrasting textures in a linear design. The arrangement of colour also contributes to the effects. Darker colours are used in the more heavily textured parts and paler colours in the smoother, lighter sections. The very shiny raffene thread and contrasting mauve threads help to draw the eye to the circle which is the focal point of the design.

When working a variety of textures in a piece of embroidery like this it is better to use a few stitches and a simple colour scheme. Too many stitches and colours can produce a confused piece of work. The stitches in this panel are variations of chain and stem stitches and the colours have been limited to tones of the background fabric, with two contrasting colours.

The heavy lines at the base of the design are in oyster chain stitch worked in handspun silk, perle cotton Nos 5 and 8 and crewel wool.

A row of Portuguese stem stitch in a shiny variegated rayon thread separates this from the lighter, smoother rows of chain stitch worked in two strands and one strand of stranded cotton.

Two more rows of Portuguese stem stitch follow, in tapestry wool, then rows of stem stitch in raffene, two strands of stranded cotton, and fine silk thread. Twisted chain and stem stitches make up the next section, in crewel wool, shiny rayon and raffene. Again Portuguese stem stitch makes a strong, heavier textured line, in perle cotton No. 5 and crewel wool. Rows of stem stitch follow, with single chains in two strands of stranded cotton making a lightly powdered effect.

The top section is worked in close rows, using whipped chain, chain and stem stitches in crewel wool, broder cotton, one strand of stranded cotton, rayon and silk threads.

The circle is worked in stem stitch with raffene, crewel wool, perle cotton No. 5 and two strands of stranded cotton. At the centre of the circle a single oyster chain stitch is worked in three strands of stranded cotton. The design is linear, with the lines forming bands or wider lines.

This design would be suitable for a tote bag. It is shown worked on a cotton fabric.

Palm Leaf (9 × 12 cm)

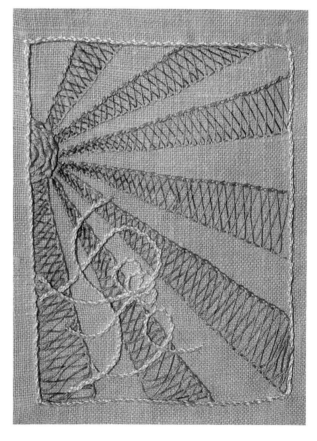

The detail photograph of a cotton palm leaf shows a contrast of very firm straight lines with fine curved lines. This has been the basis for a small embroidery, using herringbone stitch for broad straight lines, edged with twisted chain and running stitches. Two strands of stranded cotton were used in three shades of pink. The curved lines and the border were worked in whipped chain stitch with white perle cotton No. 8. The half circle is in twisted chain stitch using three strands of stranded cotton.

TEXTURE

Stitches automatically make textures. Learning to use them to create the effects you want becomes an endlessly enjoyable experience. There are infinite combinations and permutations as every different thread, size or variation of stitch will produce a different effect.

In the first row of this texture sampler are three very different textures created with Cretan stitch.

1. Worked unevenly with one strand of stranded cotton. The needle is brought out near the point where it has been taken in, at each end of the stitch. This makes a light texture very useful for shadows or softening an outline. There are three rows worked, each row encroaching into the previous row.

2. Worked in two strands of stranded cotton, very closely packed, bringing the needle out towards the middle of the stitch. This makes a much smoother texture and makes a good filling for quite a large shape.

3. Worked very openly in two strands of stranded cotton, two rows with two rows worked across them at right angles, making a cross hatched texture.

The second row is variations of buttonhole stitch.

4. Worked in shaded perle cotton No. 8 with each row exactly under the previous one. This makes a net-like texture which could also be used for roofs or parts of buildings.

5. Worked very unevenly in Danish flower thread with the stitches of succeeding rows worked between the stitches of the previous row.

6. Worked in crewel wool in short curved rows of stitches, rather uneven. The smaller rows of finer stitching are worked in one strand of stranded cotton in a contrast colour.

The third row is versions of double knot stitch.

7. Worked with shiny rayon threads in two colours, the stitches well spaced. This would make a good border.

8. Worked very densely on one side to give a very knotty texture. Where the rows of stitches have been spaced apart the texture becomes lighter, one way to achieve a shaded effect. The thread is a matt knitting cotton.

9. A much freer version of double knot stitch worked in very shiny, rather thick, rayon thread. It is unevenly spaced in curving lines.

The fourth row is variations of chain stitch.

10. Twisted chain stitch worked in velvet yarn alternately with tapestry wool, making a very close rich texture which would be good on tree trunks or areas where a dense texture is needed.

11. Rosette chain stitch, worked in perle cotton No. 5. The circular patterns have been worked with the stitches facing both inwards and outwards, giving the effect of flower forms.

12. This heavy, rough texture is created with oyster chain stitch in handspun silk thread. The unevenness of the thread adds to the texture. The central square is worked in crewel wool much more evenly to make a contrast in both colour and texture.

The sampler is worked on a moiré furnishing rayon.

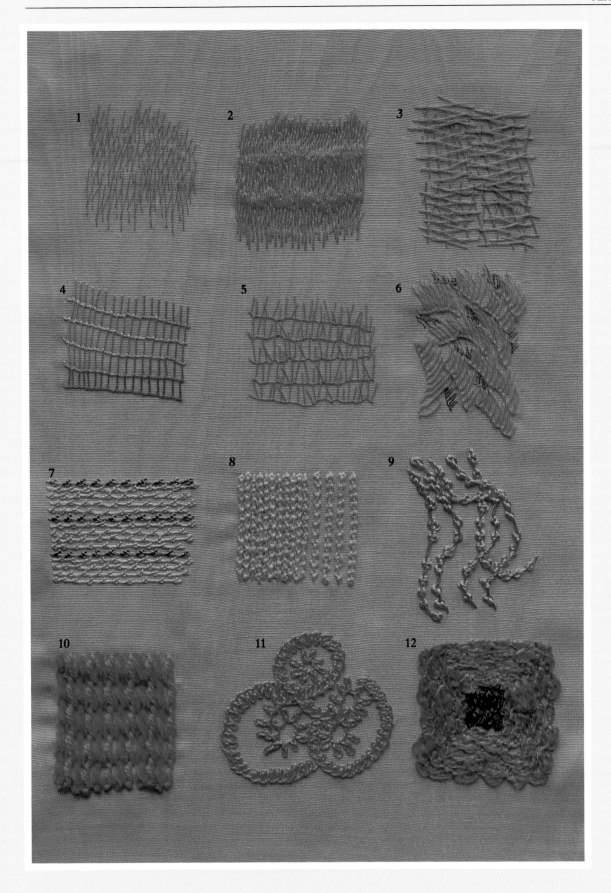

Feathers (17.9 × 29 cm)

The feathers in this embroidery are composed of very fine lines with a smooth texture, with a strong line down the centre, and a fluffy textured area at the base of each feather.

The central lines are worked in whipped chain stitch using perle cotton No. 8 in a pale stone colour. The feathers are worked in one strand of stranded cotton or fine silk thread in stem stitch. The colours range from a dark brown to light terracotta, and two shades of blue. The fluffy effect at the ends of the feathers has been achieved by using a fine angora knitting yarn and pale apricot silk thread.

This design would be suitable for a notebook cover. It is worked on a cotton fabric with a rather loose weave.

Resin (14 × 8 cm)

The textures and beautiful colours of the flow of resin from a tree make a good subject for embroidery. The flowing lines of the resin have been accentuated in the embroidery, contrasting the smoother texture at the edge with the heavy rich texture towards the centre.

The smoother texture is worked in twisted chain stitch using two strands of stranded cotton in four shades of fawn. Stronger lines are in whipped chain or Portuguese stem stitches in perle cotton No. 5.

The heavy texture is worked in oyster chain stitch in six strands of stranded cotton, floss silk and perle cotton No. 5, with some stitches in perle No. 8, and twisted chain stitch in shiny viscose thread.

The woolly sheep with its smooth nose and ridged horns is a good example of different textures and would be fun to translate into embroidery—perhaps French knots in varying sizes for the wool, stem stitch filling for the nose, and large bullion knots in various threads for the horns.

FILLING SHAPES

Points to consider when filling shapes are:
>How densely is the shape to be filled?
>Is all of the shape to be filled?
>The direction of stitching.
>The texture to be created.

Working across the rows:

1. This square is filled completely with chain stitch in perle cotton No. 8. The squares one inside the other form a pattern which catches the light on the shiny thread.

2. Worked in whipped chain using three strands of stranded cotton. There is a change of direction and colour in the lines of stitching.

3. Worked in perle cotton No. 5, partly in running stitch and partly in back stitch so that there is a contrast in texture.

4. Worked with tapestry wool couched with perle cotton No. 8, working out from the centre of the circle. Couching makes a very close dense filling.

5. Fine chain stitch in one strand of stranded cotton is worked in curved lines to give more form to the circle.

6. A more textured filling worked in alternating stem stitch in rows across the shape.

7. Stem stitch, which can be worked in a smooth thread to give a very flat finish, is shown here worked in a textured handspun silk thread. The lines of stitching follow the shape.

8. Shapes can be filled with other shapes, as this one, worked with fly stitch in perle cotton No. 8 in groups of stitches to form small triangles. The contrast colour is in silk thread.

9. Straight stitch is worked spaced apart in two strands of stranded cotton. An outline of stem stitch gives more definition to the shape.

10. Fine lines of stem stitch in one strand of a stranded rayon thread are worked closer together at one end of the oval to give a shaded effect.

11. Crewel wool is worked in herringbone stitch around the oval, the stitch at the inside of the oval being smaller than that at the outside. Sometimes a stitch had to be worked over twice at the inside to get around the curve. The centre is a contrast in colour and direction.

12. Filling a shape with other shapes again, this time with spiders' webs in perle cotton No. 5. French knots around the outline define the oval.

The sampler is worked on a furnishing rayon.

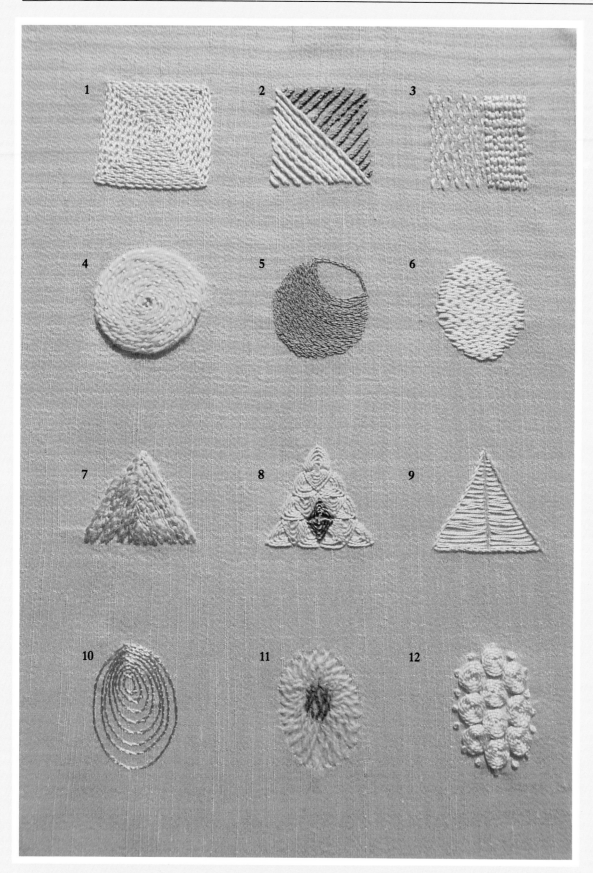

Oranges and Lemons (30 × 18 cm)

Several points need consideration before starting to fill a shape. The choice of stitch is most important as it will give texture to the shape. The direction of the stitch can add contrast to the shape, or make a pattern within it. Sometimes a change of direction can give vitality to a form which might otherwise be rather dull.

The relationship of the filled shape to the rest of the design needs to be considered. Is it a solid area in the right place? Do other shapes balance and complement it? In 'Oranges and Lemons', not all the leaves have been filled. The outlined ones tend to recede into the background. If they had all been solid the piece would have looked rather heavy.

The fruit has been worked in chain stitch to give a rather rough texture. The stitch takes a curved direction around the fruit to give roundness to the shapes. Three shades of perle cotton No. 5 have been used for both oranges and lemons, with a further shade in a shiny rayon thread.

Whipped chain stitch in linen thread is worked on the stems. The leaves are in stem stitch using three close shades of three strands of stranded cotton. The outline of the leaf and the central rib were worked first, then the lines each side of the rib. A space between these lines has been left now and again to suggest veins in the leaf.

The design is worked on linen and would be suitable for a cushion or a tablecloth, where it could be placed between each setting.

Banksia Flower (10 × 14 cm)

Banksias are a wonderful source of inspiration for embroidery design as every part of the plant has interesting forms and textures. The illustrated embroidery shows a different way of filling a shape.

Single chain stitches, worked in all directions, fill the rounded rectangular shape. Five shades of golden brown stranded cotton, used with three strands, and another shade in perle cotton No. 5, were used. Long straight stitches have been worked on top of the chain stitch filling in a variety of threads—perle No. 8, shiny rayon and silk. Only half of the flower has been completed, showing the groundwork of chain stitches. The tip is worked in French knots with brown perle cotton No. 5.

A suggestion of leaves, worked in fly stitch with linen thread, complements the heavily textured flowers.

These eucalypt buds and flowers are lovely shapes to embroider. A filling of fine chain stitches in several shades of one colour would suit the buds, with perhaps stem stitch or straight stitches for the flowers. The shades of colour and shadows on the buds would need careful study and interpretation.

LEAVES AND FOLIAGE

The examples shown here are for rather small-scale leaves. They can all be enlarged a little by making bigger stitches. All can be varied by using different threads. When working with larger leaves and foliage you can also use ideas from the previous section on filling shapes.

The top row shows four uses of single chain stitches.

1. The first example has the chain stitches placed evenly each side of a central line of stem stitch. Two strands of shaded stranded cotton have been used.
2. Worked in perle cotton No. 8, the stitches are in groups. Start with groups of three and work out from them. Each leaf is composed of two chain stitches, one inside the other.
3. The chain stitches are grouped and have long tails brought into a point. Each group is connected with a straight stitch. The thread is a twisted silk.
4. The chain stitches have been worked each side of curving lines of back stitch; each chain has a straight stitch inside it. The stitches at the tips of the sprays are in a contrasting colour. One strand of stranded cotton is used throughout.

The second row shows examples of the use of fly stitch.

5. Worked in one strand of stranded cotton; the fly stitches are uneven, with long tails, and worked over one another in groups to form a feathery effect.
6. Here the stitch is worked in vertical rows in crochet cotton No. 20.
7. The vertical rows in this version are closer together and have been worked with the outside stitch first, using perle cotton No. 5. Contrast colour on the outside of some leaves is worked in one strand of stranded cotton.
8. Small groups of fly stitches are worked in a shaded shiny rayon thread. The stalks are in chain stitch in one strand of stranded cotton.

The third row consists of variations of buttonhole stitch.

9. Worked in crewel wool in fan shapes.
10. Two rows of buttonhole stitch, worked unevenly back to back in two strands of stranded cotton. A fine stem in a contrast colour is worked in one strand.
11. A combination of straight stitch and buttonhole stitch, each leaf comprising a straight stitch and two buttonhole stitches in one strand of stranded cotton.
12. The stitch is worked around the outline of the leaf leaving a space down the centre to suggest a central rib.

The last row shows variations of Cretan stitch, with straight and stem stitches.

13. Cretan stitch worked fairly closely in perle cotton No. 5, with stems in stem stitch in two strands of stranded cotton.
14. Cretan stitch has been worked very freely in two shades of stranded cotton. Each row encroaches on the last.
15. Here are two ideas for grass. At the top, Cretan stitch, and at the bottom, straight stitch, both in two strands of stranded cotton.
16. Stem stitch is worked in crewel wool and three strands of stranded cotton, along curving lines.

The sampler is worked on a cotton and polyester fabric.

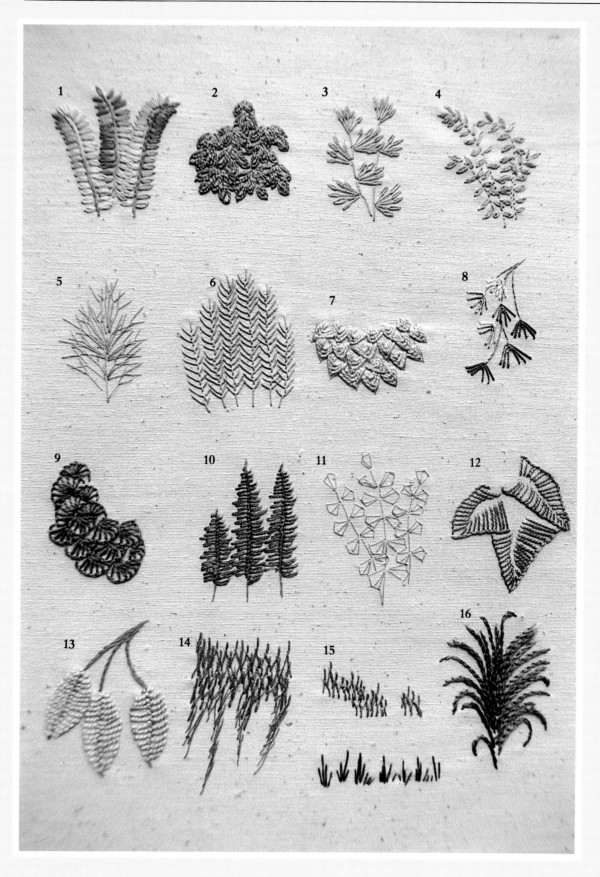

Leaves (mirror frame—24 × 30 cm)

The changing colours of leaves from spring to autumn are the basis for this design. Worked on cotton twill, the simple shapes of the leaves have been outlined in fly stitch with variegated handspun silk thread. Fly stitches in a fine silk in similar tones have been added within the outline. The central ribs are couched handspun silk.

Cretan stitch in four shades of blue has been worked very freely around the leaf shapes to suggest the seasonal colour of the sky.

The design was worked up by cutting paper shapes of leaves and arranging them in an arch shape.

Begonia Leaf (11 × 12 cm)

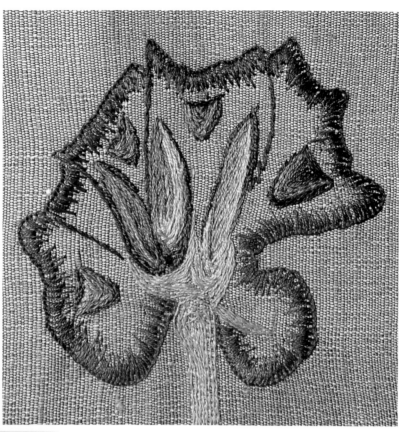

The underside of a begonia leaf has been used fairly literally in this embroidery sketch.

Worked on silk, the outline is buttonhole stitch in two strands of stranded cotton in three shades of a reddish brown. Straight stitches in one strand of stranded cotton in lighter shades and in a shiny rayon thread have been added between the buttonhole stitches. The green shapes in the leaf are filled with rows of stem stitch in two strands of stranded cotton in shaded greens. The stem is also worked in stem stitch in a pale yellow. The stitch follows the shapes of the stem and leaf ribs.

The design could be used as the pocket of a silk blouse, or perhaps repeated in slightly varying form down one side of the garment.

This rosette of young oak leaves displays interesting shapes, colour and shadows, and could be worked up into a design for a box top or bag. The leaf shapes could be filled with lines of stitches; outlined with the veins embroidered; or broken up into solid sections of stitchery.

33

ROUND FLOWERS

Flowers have inspired the decorative arts for centuries and have always been a favourite design source for embroiderers.

Flower forms are so varied it is hard to know where to begin. Notes and sketches of unusual and well loved flowering plants, their colours and forms, will prove invaluable, as will photographs. A close examination of particular flowers can reveal some surprises—of colour, shape of petals, stamens, for example. The colour of the leaves in relation to the flowers is also worth studying.

The examples in this book are just a few of the possibilities of translating flower forms into stitches. The scale of the embroidered flowers is fairly small, and could be enlarged a little if necessary. Heavier threads will work up into a larger form. If really large flowers are required, look back to the section on filling shapes.

There are endless combinations for flowers worked with circles of stitches. The obvious choices can be made more interesting by thoughtful choice of threads and colours. Several shades of colour will always give a richer effect.

1. The flowers are worked in single chains, the old lazy daisy. Each flower has five petals worked in linen thread with another chain worked within it in a different colour in two strands of stranded cotton. The centres are French knots in yet another colour, worked with perle cotton No. 5. Leaves are also single chains in groups of three using perle cotton No. 8.

2. For these flowers the single chains are worked in a fan shape to give a profile effect. A rayon thread is used, with perle cotton No. 8 worked in two straight stitches for each centre. Stems are in stem stitch in two strands of stranded cotton.

3. Shaded silk thread, worked in single oyster chains, forms the flowers. The centres are French knots in velvet yarn. Fine sprays of leaves form a contrast and are worked in stem stitch with one strand of stranded cotton.

4. These flowers are worked in herringbone stitch. The stitch has to be spread out at the outside of the flower. A ground web of stitches in a shiny rayon thread is overlaid with stitches in one strand of stranded cotton. The centres are worked in circles of back stitch in three strands of stranded cotton. Stems and leaves are worked in twisted chain stitch using three strands of stranded cotton.

5. Cretan stitch is used for the flowers, worked in perle cotton No. 8 and broder cotton. The stitch is worked closely at the centre of the flower and opened out at the outside edge. Two chain stitches in opposite directions make the centres and the stems are couched perle cotton No. 8 with leaves in fly stitches in the same thread.

6. Buttonhole stitch in groups of three forms the petals of these flowers, using perle cotton No. 5. The stitch is worked at a slight angle. The centres are three bullion knots worked in perle cotton No. 8. Stems are in back stitch using three strands of stranded cotton, with leaves formed with three fly stitches in the same thread.

7. A group of spiders' webs in three colours, worked in perle cotton Nos 5 and 8. When using several close colours in a group, make one colour predominant. In this case it is the deepest colour. The leaves are straight stitches in six strands of shaded stranded cotton.

8. Spiders' webs are used again, but this time the ground work of five stitches is in a contrast colour and the woven web does not fill the ground work. Threads used are broder cotton for the ground work and six strands of stranded cotton. Leaves are groups of fly stitches with a long tail in one strand of stranded cotton.

9. The flowers are ovals of buttonhole stitch in perle cotton No. 8 with another row of the stitch worked opposite and between the stitches of the first row in broder cotton. Clusters of French knots in perle cotton No. 8 are worked in the centre. The leaves are single chains worked alternately from the base of the group of leaves.

A cotton and polyester fabric is used for this sampler.

Bunch of Daisies (22 × 32 cm)

The daisies are worked in Cretan stitch in several different threads—white perle cotton No. 8, three strands of white stranded cotton, three strands of shaded stranded cotton, and three strands of pale grey stranded cotton. Some of the flowers are in profile or are half flowers. The flower centres are bullion knots in yellow broder cotton, yellow perle cotton No. 8 and a shiny rayon thread in an apricot colour. The leaves are worked in fly stitch, two rows around the outline, with back stitch down the centre of each leaf. One strand of soft green stranded cotton is used.

Whipped chain stitch in three strands of bright green stranded cotton forms the stems with an occasional stem in one strand of dark green stranded cotton. The soft bow is worked in rows of stem stitch with one strand of stranded cotton in two shades of deep turquoise.

The embroidery is worked on a cotton and polyester fabric and is designed as a picture.

Eucalypt Blossom (10 × 14 cm)
—Julie Wicks

Eucalypt flowers are spectacular and wonderful as a source for embroidery design.

The embroidery here is delicate. The blossom is embroidered in silk and viscose threads using back stitch, with a French knot at the end of each filament. The centres are also in back stitch, and the stems are couched handspun silk thread. Leaves are appliquéed fabric.

Hydrangeas (30 × 20 cm, detail)—Effie Mitrofanis

The flowers have been worked in chain stitches, close straight stitches and stem stitch.

There is a contrast between the filled in flowers and those left in outline. The blend of colour from quite deep red-purple to pale pink and mauve gives a richness to the work. Beads make the centres of the flowers. The leaves are worked in rows of stem stitch, using darker shades to emphasise details. The direction of the stitch gives form to the leaves.

The threads used are perle cotton No. 5, stranded cotton and broder cotton.

FLOWER SPIKES

Spikes of flowers are useful in the background of a garden scene, or in a bunch of flowers to give height.

1. Single chain stitches in broder cotton form the flower head. Each chain has a straight stitch worked inside it in a deeper shade (two strands of stranded cotton). Start working the flowers from the base with the spikes upside down, facing you. The leaves are worked in Cretan stitch in two shades of two strands of stranded cotton.

2. The flowers are worked in circles of buttonhole stitch using two strands of stranded cotton. An occasional flower is worked in shiny rayon thread. There is a French knot in perle No. 8 in the centre of each flower. The leaves are fly stitch, using two strands of shaded stranded cotton.

3. Each flower consists of eight straight stitches in crewel wool. Work stitches at north, south, east and west first, then the other four stitches between them. A small straight stitch in perle cotton No. 8 is worked at the centre of each flower. The leaves are stem stitch, worked in stranded cotton in two colours—two strands for the darker colour and one strand for the lighter.

4. The flower stems are worked in back stitch in a shiny rayon thread, with single chains for flowers in linen thread. The leaves are worked in whipped chain in perle cotton No. 5.

5. Clusters of French knots in six strands of shaded stranded cotton form the flower spikes. It is easier to work these starting from the base of the spike. The leaves are worked in buttonhole stitch in fan shapes, using two strands of stranded cotton.

6. The flower head is worked with seven rows of double knot stitch in six strands of stranded cotton. The leaves are fly stitches with long tails, worked with a shaded rayon thread.

7. There are four petals to each flower, each petal worked with two fly stitches (one inside the other) in perle cotton No. 5. There are four straight stitches in the centre in another shade of perle cotton No. 5, and a French knot right at the centre. The buds are worked with just two fly stitches. The leaves are worked with rayon thread in single chain stitches in groups of three or five.

8. The six petals of each flower are worked with pairs of fly stitches worked sideways, using perle cotton No. 8. There is a French knot at the centre of each flower worked in linen thread. Leaves are outlined in stem stitch using two strands of stranded cotton.

9. Single twisted chain stitches, worked with perle cotton No. 5, form the flower spikes, which are worked from the base up, the stitches placed closer together at the base and spaced further apart towards the top of the spike. The leaves are fly stitches, worked one underneath the other, starting at the top of the leaf with fairly small stitches and widening the stitches towards the base of the leaf. Two strands of shaded stranded cotton are used.

The background fabric is pure linen.

Lupins (42 × 52 cm)—Effie Mitrofanis

This beautiful panel started with an impression of the lupin flowers painted onto raw silk with acrylic paint. The embroidery of the flowers is in stranded cotton, perle cotton No. 5, broder cotton, shiny rayon thread and a very small amount of wool. The stitches used are French knots, bullion knots, single chains, rosette chain and herringbone stitch. Some beads have been incorporated to give extra sparkle.

The light textured buds are outlined in back stitch or running stitch. The leaves have been worked in buttonhole stitch, two rows back to back, using perle cotton No. 5 and six strands of stranded cotton. Sometimes each row is a different thread or tone.

The lower leaves have been appliquéed by machine and extend onto the silk mount.

Wisteria (18 × 25 cm)—Effie Mitrofanis

The wisteria embroidery is a richly textured combination of threads, ribbons and beads, worked on silk organza.

A pale pink knitting ribbon is used for the largest flowers, worked in varieties of chain stitches—twisted, rosette and oyster chain as well as simple single chains. Narrow satin ribbon and stranded cotton are also worked in smaller chain stitches.

Fans of buttonhole stitch in stranded cotton and perle cotton Nos 5 and 8 are interspersed with beads and French knots. Foliage is suggested with straight stitches in two strands and one strand of stranded cotton in several shades of green.

The embroidery is mounted over a piece of machine embroidered and dyed fabric, which gives the effect of flowers in the background.

Border Design (18 × 12 cm)

The flower spikes consist of single chains, each with a straight stitch worked inside it, using perle cotton Nos 5 and 8 in three shades of orange.

The daisies are worked in twisted chains, making each stitch well down the working thread and towards the centre. These are also in perle cotton No. 5 in two yellows, with French knots in a pale yellow at the centre.

White spiders' webs in perle cotton No. 5 have a yellow French knot centre. Three rosette chains in apricot perle No. 8 make the other flowers. Stems are in stem stitch and running stitch, threaded, both in perle No. 5.

Three rows of unevenly worked Cretan stitch finish the border, under the flowers. One row is in perle cotton No. 8, and two are in crochet cotton, which is also used in brown in straight stitches between the other stitches.

The border was worked on a cotton and polyester fabric for a cloth for a small table and positioned so that the lower edge of the design came to the edge of the table.

FLOWER IMPRESSIONS

The impression of a mass of flowering plants may often be more appropriate to a design than numbers of very detailed flowers.

1. Cretan stitch in three greens in two strands of stranded cotton forms the foliage, with star-like flowers scattered amongst it. These are worked in straight stitches in two yellows using one strand of stranded cotton.

2. The foliage is worked in straight stitches using perle cotton No. 5 and two strands of stranded cotton. The flowers are bullion knots in perle cotton No. 8 in two shades of orange and one of yellow.

3. This is worked entirely in straight stitches, the flowers in close stitches in five shades of mauve, using linen, rayon, stranded and perle threads. A tiny stitch in yellow forms the flower centres. The foliage is worked in three shades of green using two strands of stranded cotton.

4. The effect of a cascading mass of flowers is created by the direction of the stitches. French knots are used for the flowers, in white perle cotton No. 5 and four strands of silver-grey stranded cotton. The leaves are single chain stitches in Danish flower thread and a fine silk.

5. Close rows of double knot stitch in a circular direction suggest dense masses of flowers. They are worked in two strands of crewel wool, perle cotton No. 8 and four strands of stranded wool. Foliage is worked in linen thread in single inverted fly stitches.

6. Fly stitch is the only stitch used in this sample. The flowers are tiny stitches in all directions worked in four shades of yellow using one strand of stranded cotton and a shiny rayon thread. Impressions of leaves are made with long narrow fly stitches in four shades of green using three strands of stranded cotton.

In all of the examples it is the number of different tones of colour that give the work richness and depth.

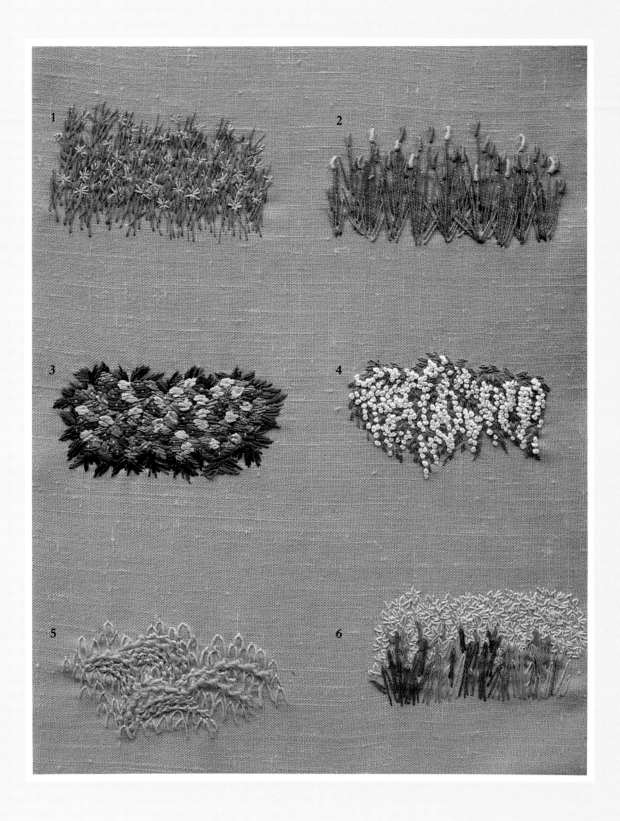

The Pergola (21 × 28 cm)—Marie Cavanagh

The linen for this embroidery was painted with fabric dye to sketch in a background.

The pergola is stitched with two strands of stranded cotton in rows of stem stitch, with the wisteria stems also in this stitch, and the flowers in tiny back stitches. The tree is worked in single chain stitches in all directions, using two strands of stranded cotton.

Rows of chain stitch in broder cotton form the pots and the border of nasturtiums has circles of buttonhole stitch for leaves with small straight stitches in red to give the impression of flowers.

Details of wall and patio are in fine stem stitch, and other details in small straight stitches.

The embroidery forms an inset panel on the flap of a large bag.

Designs inspired by the spectacular blossom of the fire-wheel tree could be embroidered in narrow ribbons, beads and line stitches such as stem, chain and whipped chain to create an impression of the rich colour and unusual form of the flowers.

Kangaroo Paws (9 × 12 cm)

The kangaroo paws have been interpreted with fly stitches in crewel wool, using three shades of orange and two shades of red. Straight stitches in perle cotton No. 8 have been added to the fly stitches. Leaves have been suggested by chain stitch in two shades of green crewel wool, and by Cretan stitch in one strand of stranded cotton in four shades of green. White French knots in perle cotton No. 8 give the impression of small flowers.

Nemesias (9 × 10 cm)—Kath Chate

The impression of these flowers is created with single chain stitches, sometimes worked with another chain inside, and buttonhole stitch. There is a row of buttonhole stitch in a fine thread over the first row.

A variety of threads include perle cotton No. 8, broder cotton, fine silk and one strand of stranded cotton. Leaves are suggested with fly stitches in twisted silk threads in several greens.

This effective embroidery could be worked on many items, as it could be adapted to to fill any shape. Table linen, boxes and clothing would all make good backgrounds for stitchery such as this.

STEMS, TRUNKS AND BRANCHES

Flower stems vary greatly and the right choice of line for the flowers you depict is important. They can be thin, thick, branching, smooth, shiny, rough, segmented and so on. As always, a study of the subject from nature will reveal many differing forms and provide much inspiration.

1. Straight stitch in shiny rayon thread.

2. Stem stitch in Danish flower thread.

3. Back stitch in two strands of stranded cotton.

4. Whipped chain in rayon thread.

5. Long chain stitches in one strand of stranded cotton.

6. Couching with six strands of stranded cotton couched with one strand.

7. Twisted chain in three strands of stranded cotton.

8. The small branches are worked with one strand of stranded cotton in fly stitch, making a long tail. Three shades are used. Other branches and the trunk are worked in straight stitches, using two strands of stranded cotton in two shades.

9. The curving branch is worked in chain stitch with stem stitch directly following it to form the finer branches. Three different weights and colours of thread are used, perle cotton No. 5, broder cotton and two strands of stranded cotton.

10. Alternating stem stitch is worked over most of this tree trunk, in two shades of perle No. 5 and dark brown perle No. 8. An occasional oyster chain stitch gives the effect of a knot on the trunk.

11. Couched handspun silk and broder cotton form the many lines on this trunk. Fine close lines of stem stitch in silk thread fill some areas, and in others herringbone stitch in the same thread gives a lighter contrast.

The sampler is worked on a cotton fabric.

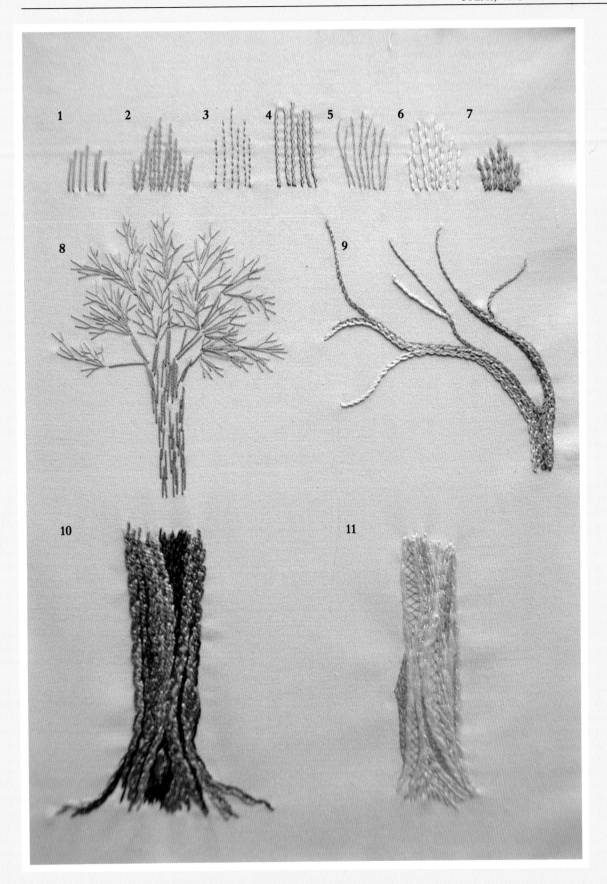

Tree Trunks (28 × 36 cm)—Kath Chate

The main tree trunk is worked in chain stitch using crewel wool and silk threads in many shades of green, fawn and cream. The direction of the stitchery gives form to the trunk and branches, with the silk thread making highlights. A heavy branch is worked in oyster and twisted chain stitches with crewel wool and a silk thread. The smaller trunk is also worked in twisted chain stitch, with a little Cretan stitch in parts of the trunk.

Plants at the base of the trees are suggested by fly stitches in single strands in greens and cream, with a strong line of couched handspun silk which has a few single oyster chains behind it worked in brown crewel wool.

The background fabric is furnishing wool.

Pothos Stems (12 × 10 cm)

The stems of an old pothos plant make a most interesting pattern.

The design has been worked mainly in stem stitch, using perle cotton No. 5, silk thread and stranded cotton, with two strands. The crescent shapes are worked in back stitch with two strands of stranded cotton. The bright greens on a white ground give a fresh appearance, and the addition of several tones of dull gold make the piece more interesting.

This design could be repeated or added to to make a border that could be used on table linen or cushions, for example.

The pattern made by this section of charred bark would be an ideal basis for a design for a belt, in various greys and silver threads, using couching, stem stitch filling or straight stitches. The variations in tone are worth studying.

TREES

The overall shape of the tree has to be studied, and the shapes made by groups of leaves. The form of the trunk and the branches, and the colours of the tree, are other points to be considered.

The six trees illustrated are all different in shape, colour and texture.

1. The trunk and branches are worked in two shades of grey with two strands of stranded cotton. The groups of leaves are worked in Cretan stitch using crewel wool, overlaid with the same stitch worked in one strand of stranded cotton. The stitch is well spaced and worked unevenly.

2. The trunk and branches are worked in chain stitch with one strand of stranded cotton; the leaves are worked in stem stitch using Danish flower thread and two strands of stranded cotton in a darker colour and one strand in a lighter shade. The heavier threads were worked first.

3. Each long weeping branch has a line of long stem stitch in perle No. 8 and three strands of stranded cotton. These lines are overlaid with uneven fly stitches in one strand of stranded cotton and a fine silk thread. The trunk is in alternating stem stitch using two strands of stranded cotton.

4. Two colours in two strands of stranded cotton are worked in a long chain stitch, following the shapes within the trees. The trunks are straight stitches in two strands of stranded cotton.

5. Single chain stitches are worked in clusters in broder cotton, two strands of stranded cotton and one strand of shiny rayon. Each cluster is completed with all the threads used before going on to the next one. Twisted chain stitch in two strands of stranded cotton forms the trunk.

6. This tree is worked entirely with straight stitches in perle cotton No. 5 and two strands of stranded cotton, and the trunk in perle cotton No. 8.

A linen and polyester fabric is the background for the sampler.

Spring Blossom (54 × 47 cm)—Doris Waltho

Layers of chiffon in pink and mauve were laid on the fabric in the shape of the tree top and held down with basting stitches.

The stitchery is in a great variety of threads: handspun silk, perle cotton Nos 3 and 5, broder cotton, rayon thread and narrow satin ribbons.

The main stitch is oyster chain in many shades of pinks, cream, mauve-red and a little green. The ribbon is worked in twisted chain in some parts as well as in oyster chain. The direction of the stitchery of the blossom gives the tree a feeling of movement.

The tree trunk is a great contrast in colour and stitchery as it is worked in fine silk threads in charcoal grey, aqua, cream and mauve, using Cretan stitch in groups.

Bush Track (36 × 30 cm)—Kath Chate

The outlines of the trees have been sensitively sketched with lines of couched handspun wool, stem stitch and twisted chain stitch in fine silk thread, using several shades of brown and cream. Leaves are suggested with Cretan stitch worked sideways in silk threads and one strand of stranded cotton, again in browns and creams.

The main tree trunk, which is the focal point of the picture, is worked in couched handspun silk in fawns. The plants and flowers that lead the eye to the tree trunk are composed of single chains in a variety of green threads and yellow French knots.

The plants at the edge of the track are in fly stitches worked in single strands in shades of soft green, cream and brown. The track is worked in browns in single strands in alternating stem stitch. Cretan stitch in browns and soft greens creates an impression of more plants in the foreground.

SKY

The treatment of the sky can help to convey the mood of an embroidery, depending on the colours used and the form of the clouds. Overworking the sky area can result in an all over textured piece of work, which may give too heavy an appearance. It is better to leave space, with just suggestions of changes in colour and cloud formations.

1. Running stitch in two strands of stranded cotton worked in rows brick fashion. A strand from each of two colours gives subtle changes of colour. The clouds are worked in a very light grey.

2. This cloud effect is in Cretan stitch, worked sideways, with one strand of stranded cotton in white and grey, two strands in cream. The rows of stitches are overlapped so that some areas become denser.

3. Fluffy angora knitting wool is couched with sewing cotton and worked in a circular direction to give the effect of tiny fluffy clouds.

4. This cloud formation is worked in chain stitch in stranded cotton, two strands, and fine silk threads. Two shades of grey, a grey-mauve and light silver grey, are used. The different weights of thread give variety to the texture of stitchery.

5. Rain clouds are suggested by slanting straight stitches of varying length worked with stranded cotton, using two strands and one strand, in three shades of grey. The rain is worked in a silver grey.

6. A sunset with the moon in the background is worked in alternating stem stitch in two shades of apricot and a mauve-grey, using one strand of stranded cotton. The moon is worked in one strand of white stranded cotton in straight stitches.

The sampler is worked on a cotton and polyester fabric.

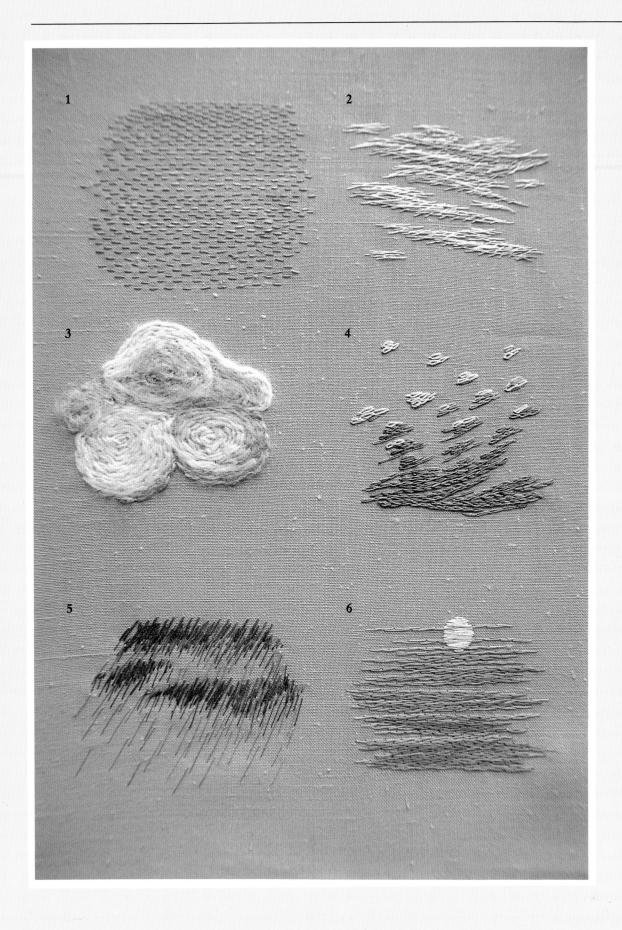

Sunrise (20 × 14 cm)

This embroidery was inspired by the spectacular sunset in the photograph. The subject has been simplified, with the tree shapes stylised and fewer clouds. Orange silk was chosen for the background. The trees and horizontal lines are worked in two shades of a dark purple-grey handspun silk, using continuous couching. The couching thread is matching sewing cotton.

The sky and deep yellow sunrise are worked in long straight stitches in one strand of shiny rayon and stranded cotton. The colours shade from a deep apricot and bright yellow at the horizon to deep orange and light red at the top.

The clouds are worked in twisted chain stitch, in fine silk at the horizon, gradually working in darker colours in stranded cotton, and two strands of silk for the heavy clouds at the top.

New Zealand Sky

(13 × 10 cm)

The sky is in Cretan stitch, working the stitch sideways and rather irregularly. White, off white and two shades of grey are used with one strand of stranded cotton. The mountains are suggested in back stitches with perle cotton No. 8. Straight stitches in one strand of stranded cotton form the shadows under the

mountains. The water is worked in stem stitch in close rows with two strands of stranded cotton, with an occasional darker line in one strand.

   This would make a very nice greetings card or small picture.

A sky with billowy clouds complements this landscape. This sky might best be interpreted in couched mohair knitting wool, with the occasional short row of twisted chain stitch. There are many shades of grey in the clouds, which would repay careful study.

WATER

Water varies tremendously and offers wonderful subjects for embroidery. A still pond of greens and browns, a waterfall over dark rocks, a torrent of rain over part of a landscape, a surging sea with surf are just some ideas depicted here.

1. A pond worked in stem stitch using three strands of stranded cotton in four shades of green and perle cotton No. 8 in turquoise. The stitchery takes a circular direction. The clumps of reeds are straight stitches in three strands of stranded cotton.

2. A stretch of sea in shallow, open herringbone stitch, worked rather unevenly. Three rows of varying length in deep blue perle cotton No. 8 were worked first. These rows were overlaid with others, also of various lengths, in three blues and two greens, using two strands of stranded cotton. The white stitches, in one strand of stranded cotton, were worked last. The variety of colours and uneven stitching creates the effect.

3. The wave is worked first, in whipped chain stitch making a heavy line. The areas between are filled with rows of stem stitch. The threads are perle cotton Nos 3 and 8, broder cotton and stranded cotton, used with one and two strands. The colours vary from deep blue to a yellow-green, and there are eight different colours in the wave. The underneath of the wave is mostly blue and darker in tone than the top of the wave, where greens predominate. The white surf is worked in very uneven buttonhole stitch, using one strand of stranded cotton in white and cream.

4. A waterfall worked in long chain stitches in one strand of stranded cotton in white, cream and pale green. The chain stitches are interspersed with double knot stitch, leaving a long space between the knots. Straight stitches form the rocks, in two strands of stranded cotton, and the surf is worked in single chains and French knots, using two strands of stranded cotton.

5. The outline of the fountain is in stem stitch, using three strands of stranded cotton, with the front edge of the bowl in Portuguese stem stitch. The fountain is in twisted chain stitch, using broder cotton, and running stitch in one strand of stranded cotton. The water in the bowl is suggested by straight horizontal stitches. The overflowing water is worked in stem and running stitches in blue and white stranded cotton, one strand.

6. The still water is suggested by lines of alternating stem stitch in three blues and a yellow-green, worked in one strand of stranded cotton. The reeds are straight stitches in three greens, using two and one strand of stranded cotton. The reflections are worked in back stitch with one strand of stranded cotton.

The background fabric is a linen and polyester mixture.

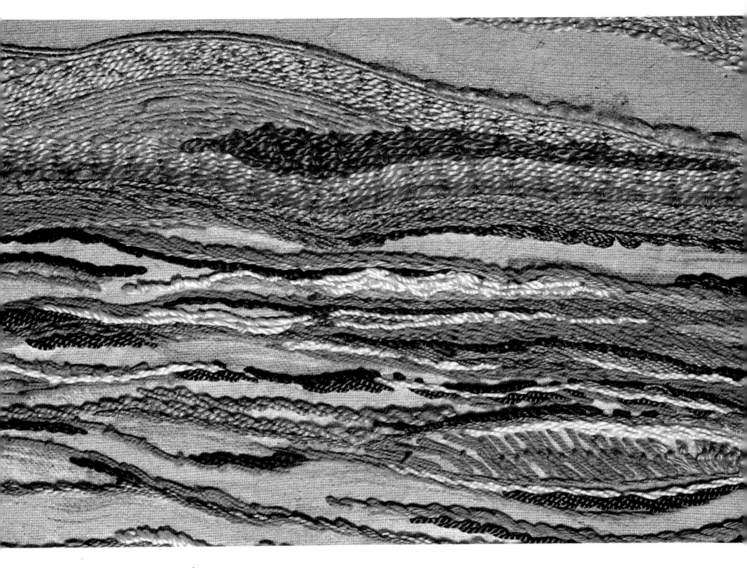

Rough Water (14 × 9 cm)—Adrienne Allen

The design of this piece was sketched onto cotton calico with watercolour pencils. The only two stitches used are couching and stem stitch.

The hills of the background are couched in soft cotton, perle cotton No. 5 and handspun silk in shades of blue, from a dark colour to a bright blue. The variety of threads makes the contrasts of texture.

The water is worked mainly in stem stitch in four strands of stranded cotton, perle cotton No. 5, Danish flower thread and a shiny rayon thread which is also couched to form highlights on the water.

Although this is only a small embroidery it has a strong design that carries well, mainly effected through the use of colour. The dark blue lines in the water and highlights of shiny cream help to give the impressions of a wind-whipped stretch of water.

Ornamental Stream (9 × 13 cm)

The smooth water is conveyed by alternating stem stitch worked horizontally in one strand of stranded cotton in four shades of green with highlights in a shiny viscose thread.

Foliage is worked in twisted chain, Cretan and fly stitches, using a variety of threads—linen, perle cotton No. 8, Danish flower thread, wool and stranded cotton.

This small picture could be framed with a dark green mount and wood frame.

The contrast between the dark rocks and creamy frothy water would be exciting to stitch. The rocks are matt and could be embroidered in straight stitches in wool and dull cotton threads, whereas the turbulent water needs knotty and textured stitches like double knot or oyster chain in a variety of cream and white threads.

BUILDINGS

There is endless inspiration for design in buildings, whether using repeated outlines or details, pictorial views, unusual aspects or parts such as windows or doors.

1. The outline of the roof is in whipped chain using two strands of stranded cotton. One strand is used for the back stitched outline of the walls. Tiles on the roof have been suggested by uneven rows of buttonhole stitch, and bricks in the walls with straight stitches, both in one strand of stranded cotton. The windows are couched perle cotton No. 8 and the door is worked in straight stitches with two strands of stranded cotton. The outline of the patio is in stem stitch.

2. The corrugated iron roof of the cottage is worked in stem stitch in grey stranded cotton, two strands for the outline and one strand for the lines of the corrugated iron. Chimneys are in stem and straight stitches in two strands of stranded cotton. The outline of the house is in alternating stem stitch using two strands of stranded cotton. Brown perle cotton No. 8 is couched for the outline of the verandah and its posts. Straight stitches in white perle cotton No. 8 outline the windows, and glass is suggested by slanting straight stitches in one strand of grey stranded cotton. The outline of the door is in stem stitch, with details in straight stitches and a French knot for the door handle.

3. The outline of the terrace house is worked in Portuguese stem stitch in perle cotton No. 3. Doors and windows have been worked in broder cotton in stem and straight stitches. The cast iron at the top of the house is in rosette chain stitch with a French knot at the end of every chain, and buttonhole stitch worked between the top of every stitch. Perle cotton No. 8 is the thread used. Also in perle cotton No. 8 are the two iron balcony rails, worked in running stitch which has been laced with another thread and caught down with a small stitch. Single chains are worked over each running stitch, and in groups to form the corner brackets.

4. A group of three quite different terrace houses which form a nice pattern. Six strands of stranded cotton are couched at the sides of the houses. The gables are in brown crewel wool using three large fly stitches, with a bullion knot at the top. The roofs are in alternating stem stitch using two strands of grey stranded cotton. The same stitch in brown handspun silk thread is used for the wall at the base of the houses. Details of windows, doors and chimneys are worked in straight stitches in two strands of stranded cotton in blue and grey.

5. A stylised cityscape worked in shades of aqua and grey. Straight stitches, in crewel wool or stranded cotton, are worked across the shapes, then overlaid with couched threads of varying thickness, or stem stitch. Changes of direction in the stitchery give variety.

6. A glasshouse in a botanic garden is worked mainly in straight stitches and couching, with stem stitch for the details of the arched window. The top of the building is worked in herringbone stitch, one end of the stitches worked over the same spot each time. A row of double knot stitch is worked

underneath. Slanting straight stitches in grey are worked in groups across the centre section to suggest reflections in the glass. Threads used are perle cotton Nos 8 and 12 and one strand of stranded cotton.

The sampler is worked on a polyester fabric.

The Homestead (27 × 20 cm)—Doris Waltho

The calico background for the embroidery has been painted with fabric dye to give colour to the sky, foreground and house details. The iron roof is created with straight stitches in grey and rust colours using three strands of stranded cotton. The filigree iron on the verandah is chain stitch with a French knot.

The impression of a flower border has been created with Cretan stitch in green stranded cotton and French knots for flowers in perle cotton No. 5. The fence in the foreground is made up of long straight stitches in a grey matt knitting ribbon and long stitches in perle cotton No. 3. The long grass in the foreground is worked in straight stitches in shades of tan and green in perle cotton No. 5.

The leaves of the trees are fly stitches in various shades of green stranded cotton used with both two and one strands.

Terrace Houses (30 × 24 cm)—Doris Waltho

Each house is worked in a variety of chain, buttonhole and Cretan stitches, with the top outline in chain stitch and double knot stitch. The railings are back stitched, with groups of single chain stitches.

The threads include tapestry wool, perle cotton No. 5, broder cotton, linen thread and stranded cotton in a harmonious blend of colours from terracotta to pink and grey. The Cretan stitch in one strand of stranded cotton makes a nice contrast to the heavier stitches.

Wellington Houses (18 × 14 cm)—Doris Waltho

The houses nestling among trees on a hillside make an appealing pattern. The roofs are worked in alternating stem stitch with one strand of stranded cotton. The walls are in twisted chain stitch, which gives a nice texture. The stitch is worked very long and the direction is changed for some walls. Other details are in straight stitches. The foliage consists of fly stitch and single chains in two strands and one strand of stranded cotton and a shiny viscose thread.

This view of an old verandah could be the basis of a very interesting design. The lines of the roof, walls and floor all run in different directions and the doors make a break in the lines of the wall. The combination of colours, from greys to golden yellows, is soft but rich.

STITCH PATTERNS

Making patterns with stitches is not at all difficult. Two rows of any stitch, worked in different threads and shades of colour, will make a pattern that can be added to. It is the combinations of threads and colours as well as stitches that will make the patterns interesting and vibrant. Stitch patterns can be used in clothing, cushions, frame borders, table linen, belts and bags.

1. This pattern comprises two rows of running stitch in a glittery knitting yarn, threaded in a circular direction with tapestry wool. Each loop of the threaded wool is held down with a chain stitch in perle cotton No. 5 and there are French knots in shiny rayon thread down the centre of the pattern.

2. Widely spaced herringbone stitch in mauve velvet yarn is the basis of the pattern. Two more rows of herringbone are worked over the first one, each one a little further into the centre, in two shades of blue perle cotton No. 5. Spiders' webs are worked in the spaces in the same blue threads, half the row in the darker colour and half in the lighter shade. French knots in yellow and dark red perle cotton add contrast to the pattern.

3. Double knot stitch in red perle cotton No. 5 is worked at the centre of the pattern, then fly stitch in red silk, three stitches worked one underneath the other between each of the buds. Another row of fly stitch is added between the previous rows with a chain stitch at the end of each stitch. Dark red perle cotton No. 8 is used.

4. Groups of three Cretan stitches, worked so that the tops of the stitches are uneven, make this pattern. The threads are blue stranded cotton, three strands, and purple and mauve linen thread. Single chains in yellow are worked each side of the pattern to give some contrast.

5. This is a very free pattern of curving lines. The heavy lines were worked first, in Portuguese stem stitch with tapestry wool and a shiny rayon thread. The finer lines are in stem stitch using a dark red perle cotton No. 8. Small spiders' webs in a glittery knitting yarn are worked in spaces made by the intersecting lines.

6. This pattern has been created with straight stitches and bullion knots. Four straight stitches in blue perle cotton No. 5 form the sides of the square. Two shades of blue are used. The centres are bullion knots in mauve linen thread, with a straight stitch in red perle silk No. 5 right in the middle. A straight stitch in golden yellow perle cotton No. 8 has been added to each square, alternately at top and bottom of the pattern.

The background fabric is linen and polyester.

Waistcoat

This waistcoat is made of handwoven natural wool and lined with silk.

The pattern consists of two rows of running stitch, in handspun natural wool, threaded in a circular direction and each loop held down with single chain stitch in handspun silk thread. The alternate stitches at the end of each chain are long, and the shorter stitches have a cream French knot at the end.

Down the centre of the two rows of this pattern are crossed straight stitches in mauve tapestry wool alternating with a large French knot in cream perle cotton No. 3 used double.

Between the rows of the running stitch pattern are four straight stitches in a cross in mauve tapestry wool, with four straight stitches in blue crewel wool from each corner, with a French knot at the end in deep blue acrylic knitting yarn.

PATTERNS FROM NATURE

Patterns in a natural form are never absolutely regular and this is part of their charm. The study of a particular natural object can result in some wonderful ideas for embroidery designs. Preparations for a piece of embroidery are most important and should include drawings and/or photographs, samples of fabric and stitches and a colour scheme. The finished work will have much more depth and feeling as a result. A series of embroideries worked up from an in-depth study of a favourite subject is an absorbing and exciting project to work on.

The close-up of a red-hot poker flower has been translated into a small embroidered sketch (8 × 6 cm). Groups of four or five buttonhole stitches, uneven and forming a rounded end to each small section, have been worked in two strands of stranded cotton, broder cotton and perle cotton No. 8. The colours are those of the flower, shading from deep pink to pale yellow, with four shades of each colour. Straight stitches have been added into spaces in the buttonhole stitches, and also at the top of each section, in a shiny rayon shaded thread.

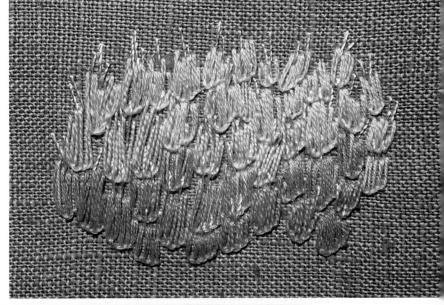

The idea could be worked in a border and used on table linen or small items such as needle cases, glasses cases and pincushions.

The design of flowers is worked on a linen tea towel. Each flower is different, although similar. The outlines are worked in stem stitch in white perle cotton No. 5 and the stamens in long chain stitches in one strand of shaded green stranded cotton.

Honesty (14 × 20 cm)
—Doris Waltho

This is a detail of an attractive design for a circular tablecloth, worked in simple stitches.

The stems are worked in double knot stitch, in perle cotton No. 5 in two shades of grey. The honesty seeds are in perle cotton Nos 5 and 8 in white, cream and fawn. The stitch used is buttonhole, with some straight stiches in between the buttonhole stitches and at the end of the seeds.

The close up of foxglove flowers reveals beautiful shapes which could be used for an exciting design.

Rocks and stones are good sources for designs, particularly linear ones. The agate illustrated has strong lines and areas of texture that would translate well into stitchery.

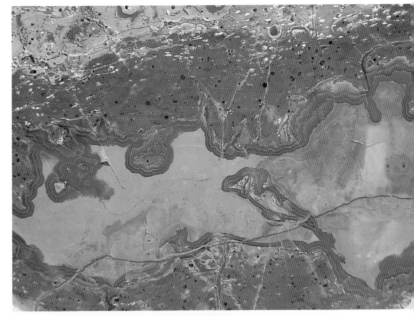

Shells are superb examples of design, combining form and pattern very successfully. The spiral on top of this shell would make a good design for a cushion or bag. The other view combines lovely curves and broken lines that suggest running stitch.

Seeds are further examples of wonderful shapes and patterns. The irregular pattern of seed cases on the banksia would be terrific on a belt in rather raised stitchery.

79

GETTING IT ALL TOGETHER

The first thing to decide when you begin a project is the size and shape of the object to be embroidered. Your design can then be worked up to fit the required space precisely.

The design itself comes next. Usually an idea for a design is already in the back of one's mind, be it flowers, landscape, geometric shapes or whatever. Make a study of the subject, with photographs, drawings, collections of magazine pictures. Everything helps. If possible photograph the source yourself and/or make drawings from it. Make notes about colours in the original, finding coloured paper or painting patches to match them.

Working up a design with cut paper shapes is very satisfactory as the shapes can be moved about, re-cut or trimmed very quickly. Lines can be added to complete the design. Once a satisfactory design is achieved, glue the shapes in place and make sure all outlines and lines are clearly marked with a black felt pen. Then make a photocopy, which can be used to transfer the design to fabric.

Only transfer what is absolutely necessary. Sometimes you will only need to mark in the centres of flowers, or a horizon line. It is often quite enough to have your original design to refer to while working. A much freer and more lively piece of work will result.

To transfer a design or part of a design, trace the outlines onto nylon net with a fairly thick felt pen. Pin or tape the net into place on the fabric and, working on a flat surface, trace the outlines with a hard sharp pencil or chalk pencil. A dotted line will then be marked around the outlines on the fabric.

Next, gather together all the threads you think you will need. Plan the colour proportions. One colour should predominate. If all the colours in a piece are in the same proportion and intensity it will look dull. A small amount of a contrast colour can work wonders. Several tones or shades of colour will always look richer than just one tone. Look at examples in this book and see how many tones are used in various parts of an embroidery. Remember that the colour of the fabric is part of the colour scheme.

The things to avoid in a design include:
Shapes all the same size or evenly spaced
Too many different shapes
Strong lines leading off the design
Too many textures (i.e. stitches)
Too many colours
Equal proportions of colour

One of the most common faults in design is the lack of a focal point. Make sure your design has a definite focal area. This can be emphasised with colour, lines leading to it or around it, larger shapes or spaces. Learn to look at the spaces in a design and assess whether they are a pleasing shape and sufficiently varied in size.

It all takes experience. Start with something fairly small, with a simple design and colour scheme. Stitch patterns are easy to work up, and look good on a needle case, which is a very useful acquisition.

Do not expect a perfect result the first time. Practice *does* make perfect. Stitching is a very pleasurable pastime and should be enjoyed!

DESIGNS

'Bunch of Daisies'—for details
of stitches and threads see page 37.

'Oranges and Lemons'—see pages 28 and 29 for colour illustration with stitch and thread descriptions.

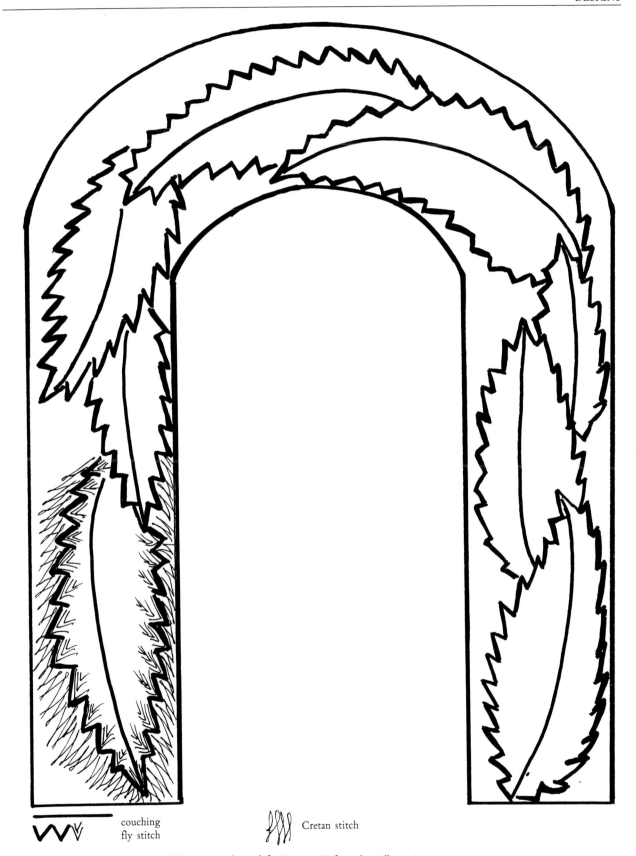

couching
fly stitch

Cretan stitch

'Mirror Frame' Repeat stitches for all leaves as in lower left. See page 32 for colour illustration.

'Pothos Stems'—for details of stitches and threads see page 57.

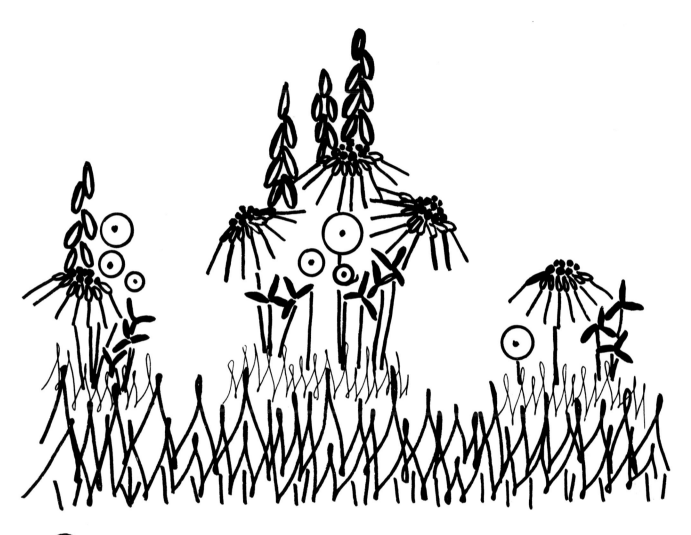

 spider's web

French knots

twisted chain with long stem

rosette chain

straight stitch

Cretan stitch

 single chains with a straight
stitch inside

'Flower Border'—see page 46 for colour illustration and thread description.

 stem stitch in perle cotton No. 5

long chain stitch in one strand of stranded cotton

French knots in perle cotton No. 5

'Border'—see page 77 for colour illustration.

INDEX